NAHC
Wild Game Cookbook

Edited by
Mike Vail

North American Hunting Club
Minneapolis, Minnesota

Acknowledgements

We would like to thank the following for their help:

NAHC Members, for sending us their delicious, original wild game recipes that serve as the foundation of the 1997 NAHC Wild Game Cookbook. These recipes – recommended by your fellow NAHC Members – are certain to delight.

NAHC staff members, for their diligence, patience and hard work in seeing to the preparation off a useful and readable cookbook of which the NAHC's members can be proud. They include Book Products Development Manager Steve Perlstein and Book Development Coordinator Dan Kennedy.

Book Design by Zins Design Studio

*Please address reprint requests
and orders for additional cookbooks to:*
NAHC Cookbook Editor
P.O. Box 3401
Minneapolis, MN 55343

CONTENTS

Cookbook Abbreviations

tsp. = teaspoon
T. = tablespoon
pt. = pint
oz. = ounce
pkg. = package
qt. = quart

Measurement Conversions

1 pinch = less than ⅛ tsp.
1 T. = 3 tsp.
2 T. = 1 oz.
4 T. = ¼ cup
5 T + 1 tsp. = ⅓ cup
8 T. = ½ cup
16 T. = 1 cup

1 cup = 8 oz.
1 pint = 16 oz.
1 quart = 32 oz.
1 gallon = 128 oz.

1 cup = ½ pint
2 cups = 1 pint
4 cups = 1 quart
2 pints = 1 quart
4 pints = ½ gallon
8 pints = 1 gallon
4 quarts = 1 gallon
8 gallons = 1 bushel

Introduction
Cooking Game Over a Live Fire

A. Cort Sinnes

There is something right and natural about cooking game over a live fire. Sure, there are excellent recipes for stove-top preparations of game, but game—be it pheasant, duck, elk, or venison—gain an added measure of authenticity when it's charcoal grilled or roasted. That said, make no mistake about it: Cooking game over a live charcoal fire is one of the trickiest of all cooking methods to get right. So when you do it well, give yourself a pat on the back, with the knowledge that you've accomplished quite a feat.

Why is wild game so difficult to cook successfully over a bed of coals? Simply put, most wild game is much, much leaner than the domesticated equivalents found at the butcher shop and, generally speaking, tougher, unless it has been properly aged. Any home cook can get around these two facts by employing a couple of time-honored outdoor cooking techniques, namely indirect cooking and marinating. But before going into importance of those two practices, here's a charcoal cooking checklist to get you off on the right foot:

1 Allow food to just come to room temperature before grilling. Generally speaking, this means removing it from the refrigerator approximately 30 minutes prior to cooking.

2 Clean out the bottom of the grill before you start a new batch of coals so air can freely circulate through the draft holes.

3 Plan on 30 to 40 minutes from lighting the fire to having charcoal that's ready for grilling—when the fire has burned down and the coals are covered with a fine, gray ash. As appealing as those pictures are of game being cooked over

a flaming fire, flames are the surest route to ruining any meat—whether it's from a hunting trip or the local butcher. Fat dripping down into live flames produces an acrid smoke that has ruined more than one grilled meal. Perhaps the greatest chef of all time, Auguste Escoffier, wrote: "Whatever fuel is used in grills, it is essential that it produce no smoke, for if smoke either from fuels used or from the falling of fat from cooking is allowed to bathe the food, it will surely acquire a disagreeable taste."

4 Always use the best quality charcoal available. Budget brands cause more problems than the cost savings justify.

5 Always put the cooking grill in place over the hot coals for a few minutes before putting the food on. As an extra precaution against foods sticking to the grill, brush it with vegetable oil.

Indirect Cooking

When you cook food on a covered grill using the indirect method, you are, in effect, charcoal *roasting* rather than charcoal *grilling*. Not only do a majority of foods turn out better this way (as opposed to cooking directly over the coals), an added and important benefit is achieved, namely, the elimination of fat dripping from the meat onto the coals, with the negative results mentioned above.

Indirect cooking is reserved for large cuts of meat or whole poultry (whether butterflied or not). This is the method meats were cooked for countless generations prior to the invention of the electric or gas oven, and prior to that, the coal oven. To achieve this timeless method of producing excellent roasted game, you'll need a covered grill. Once the coals are fired up and covered with a light gray ash, position them in equal piles, on opposite sides of the fire grate, leaving the center of the grate free of coals. If a marinade has been used, wipe the meat or poultry dry (otherwise it won't brown properly) before searing it quickly, directly over one of the piles of coals. Watch this searing process like a hawk and don't let any flames form. The object is to nicely brown all sides of whatever it is you're cooking, quickly. Once the food has been seared, insert a meat thermometer into the thickest portion of the meat, position the roast, or what have you, in the middle of the cooking grate, and put the lid in place, with the top and bottom vents completely open. Keep a close eye on thermometer, removing the meat when it's about 5 degrees shy of the desired temperature. Place the meat on a carving board, tent with aluminum foil, and allow to rest for 10-15 minutes, during which time it will come up to the desired temperature.

Marinades

Don't make the mistake so many home cooks make, thinking that marinades are simply a way to add flavor to a food. Although there are exceptions, when cooking wild game you don't want to mask or overwhelm the flavor of the game but, rather, enhance it. Consider marinating game almost a necessity: the use of mild-flavored marinade will make up for the natural leaness of the meat and slightly tenderize it in the process. Marinating adds moisture deep inside the meat that mere basting cannot. Generally speaking, you should marinate game overnight, in the refrigerator.

GRILLED QUAIL WITH PANCETTA

8-12 quail
      olive oil
      fresh lemon juice
      dried thyme leaves, crumbled
      salt and freshly ground pepper
8-12 thin slices of pancetta

Start the charcoal (approximately 60 briquettes or like-sized pieces of lump charcoal). Put the cooking grill in place so it has a chance to heat up thoroughly before you grill the quail.

While the charcoal is taking off, flatten the quail by splitting them up the backbone (a pair of poultry shears makes easy work of this). After splitting them, set the quail skin side up on the cutting board and flatten them, using the heel of your hand. Expect some of the small bones to break in the process. Flattening the quail (indeed, any poultry or game bird) makes them far easier to handle on the grill.

Rinse the quail in cold water and pat dry. Rub each quail with a little olive oil and fresh lemon juice, and then sprinkle each one with the thyme, salt, and freshly ground pepper. Wrap each quail with a slice of pancetta; hold the pancetta in place with a toothpick, if desired. Place quail on a platter, ready for the grill.

When the coals have reached the white-hot stage and are evenly covered with a fine, white ash, arrange them in an even layer with the sides touching. Position the quail directly over the coals, skin side up. The quail cook in a total of just 7-10 minutes, depending on their size, so you'll want a hot fire to produce a crispy skin in a hurry. Grill, skin side up, for approximately 3-4 minutes. Turn quail and cook for an additional 4-5 minutes, being careful not to let them burn. Serve hot off the grill, or at room temperature.

Serves 4.

GRILLED DUCK WITH ROSE AND ROSEMARY

For the marinade:

 $^2/_3$ cup rose wine
 $^1/_4$ cup olive oil
    juice of $^1/_2$ lemon
2-3 cloves garlic, minced
 $1^1/_2$ tsp. dried rosemary, crushed
    freshly ground pepper, to taste

 1 4-5 lb. duck, cut into serving pieces

Combine all ingredients for the marinade in a container and mix well. Wash the duck pieces in cold water and pat dry. Place in the marinade, cover, and refrigerate for 2-3 hours, turning twice.

Start the charcoal (approximately 60 briquettes). Give the grill a chance to heat up before grilling the meat. At the same time you start the coals, remove the duck from the refrigerator and thaw to room temperature.

When the coals have reached the white-hot stage and are evenly covered with a fine, white ash, arrange them into equal amounts and push to opposite sides of the fire grate. Position a disposable aluminum drip pan in the center of the fire grate. Replace the cooking grate.

Place duck pieces (reserving the breasts until later) directly over the drip pan. Cover grill, keeping the top and bottom vents completely open. Total cooking time for the legs and wings will be approximately 40 minutes; individual breast's will cook in 10-14 minutes, depending on the size. Keep a close watch on the clock, and put the breast's on 25-30 minutes into the cooking process. Turn the pieces every 10 minutes. If the duck has not browned to your liking after about 30 minutes, move directly over the coals for the last 5-10 minutes.

On an open grill, cook the duck (except breasts) directly over the coals. Starting skin side down, grill for 5 minutes. Turn and cook 6-8 minutes longer, basting with the marinade. Continue this process for a total of 30-45 minutes. Breast portions cook in just 10-14 minutes. Be careful not to overcook the duck; the meat should be moist.

Serves 2 to 4 people.

GRILLED BUTTERFLIED PHEASANT

Note: The only suitable wild pheasant for grilling are young birds. A good indicator of youth is a pliable breastbone and the very distinctive first wing-tip feather: In a young pheasant it is pointed; in an older bird it is rounded. Save older, tougher pheasant for moist-heat, stove-top cooking.

   1   pheasant, about 2-3 lbs.
        vegetable oil
   2   tsp. powdered sage
        salt and freshly-ground black pepper, to taste

Start the charcoal (approximately 50 briquettes or like-sized pieces of lump charcoal). Put the cooking grill in place so it has a chance to heat up thoroughly before you grill the quail.

While the charcoal is taking off, butterfly or flatten the pheasant by splitting it up the backbone (a pair of poultry shears makes easy work of this). After splitting it, set the pheasant skin side up on the cutting board and flatten it, using the heel of your hand and considerable, sharp pressure. Expect some of the small bones to break in the process. Flattening the pheasant (indeed, any poultry or game bird) makes it far easier to handle on the grill.

Rinse the pheasant in cold water and pat dry. Rub the pheasant all over with vegetable oil, and then sprinkle with the sage, salt, and freshly ground pepper.

When the coals have reached the white-hot stage and are evenly covered with a fine, white ash, arrange them in an even layer with the sides touching. The pheasant cooks in a total of just 12-15 minutes, so you'll want a hot fire to produce a crispy skin in a hurry. Grill directly over the coals, breast side down, for approximately 5-8 minutes. Turn quail and cook for an additional 5-8 minutes, being careful not to let it burn. Serve hot off the grill.

Serves 2

MIKE'S WELL-SEASONED BACKSTRAP FILLETS

For the marinade:

- ⅓ cup Worcestershire sauce
- ⅓ cup dry red wine
- 3 T. olive oil
- 2 T. balsamic vinegar
- 2 cloves garlic, pressed
- 2 tsp. dried oregano
- 1 fresh serrano chile, seeded, and finely chopped
  freshly ground black pepper

- 8 venison backstrap fillets, about 1" thick

Combine all the ingredients for the marinade in a shallow container and mix well. Place the venison fillets in the marinade, cover, and refrigerate for 2 to 3 hours, turning once or twice.

Start the charcoal (approximately 60 briquettes or like-sized pieces of lump charcoal). Put the cooking grill in place so it has a chance to heat up thoroughly before you grill the meat. At the same time as you start the coals, remove the venison fillets from the refrigerator and allow to come to room temperature.

When the coals have reached the white-hot stage and are evenly covered with a fine, white ash, arrange them in an even layer with the sides touching. Back in the kitchen, place the marinated fillets on a platter, ready for the grill, and dust with additional freshly ground pepper on both sides.

Position the fillets directly over the coals and cook approximately 3 minutes. Turn the fillets once, using a thin-bladed spatula or tongs and cook for an additional 3 minutes. Serve hot off the grill.

Serves 8 as an appetizer; 4 as a main dish.

SALT-ENCRUSTED ELK STEAK

For the marinade:

- 2 cups dry red wine
- 1/3 cup olive oil
- 1/2 tsp. thyme
- 2 bay leaves
  salt and freshly ground pepper to taste

- 1 large elk steak, about 4 lbs., in one piece, about 2-2 1/2" thick
- 4-5 lbs. table salt
- 2 large brown grocery bags

Combine marinade ingredients in a shallow container and mix well. Place the elk steak in the marinade, cover, and refrigerate for 2-3 hours.

Start the charcoal (approximately 65-75 briquettes). Remove the elk steak from the marinade and wipe dry. Wet the paper bags thoroughly and nest one inside the other to form a double bag.

Moisten the salt with water to form a thick paste. With the wet bags on a flat surface, spread a layer of wet salt, about 1-1½ inches thick, on the bottom of the bag and place the steak on the salt. Cover the steak with another layer of salt, 1-1½ inches thick, packing salt around the edges of the steak. Fold the bag tightly to form a neat, compact package.

When the coals are white-hot, and are evenly covered with a fine, white ash, place the bagged steak directly on the coals and cover with an additional layer of hot coals, at least three inches thick.

Allow the bagged steak to cook undisturbed for 30 minutes if you like your steak rare; 35-45 minutes if you prefer medium-rare to medium. Under no circumstances should you cook the steak for longer than 45 minutes.

When the steak has cooked for the desired length of time, scrape away the top layer of coals, and lift out the steak with a long pair of sturdy tongs or a flat shovel. Remove whatever paper may still be left, and crack away the salt crust. Place the steak on a platter for slicing.

Serves 8.

GRILLED TURKEY MOLE

For the mole marinade:

8   T. mild chile powder
1   cup apple cider vinegar
$1/2$ Mexican chocolate tablet (or $1/2$ cup melted, unsweetened, dark baking chocolate plus a dash of cinnamon)
$1/2$ tsp. oregano
2   cloves garlic, pressed
1   tsp. ground cumin
$1/2$ tsp. salt
$1/4$ tsp. ground black pepper

1   squab turkey, cut into serving pieces

Combine marinade ingredients in a medium saucepan. Cook over medium heat until ingredients are well-blended. Remove the pan from the stove and allow marinade to cool.

Pour the cooled marinade into a non-reactive container; add turkey pieces. Cover and refrigerate overnight.

Start the charcoal (approximately 60 briquettes). Give the grill a chance to heat up thoroughly before you grill the meat. When you start the coals, remove the turkey from the refrigerator and allow to come to room temperature.

If you have a covered grill, when the coals have reached the white-hot stage and are evenly covered with a fine, white ash, arrange them in a pile in the center of the fire grate. Put the cooking grate back in place.

Place the turkey pieces in a circle around the bed of coals, but not directly over them. Cover the grill, keeping both the top and bottom vents completely open. Total cooking time will be approximately 50-60 minutes. Turn the pieces every 10 minutes. If they have not browned to your liking after about 30 minutes, move directly over the coals for the last 5-10 minutes.

If you have an open grill, cook the turkey pieces, starting skin side down, for 8 minutes. Turn and cook for an additional 6-8 minutes, basting with the marinade, if desired. Continue to repeat this process for a total cooking time of 50-60 minutes. Keep a water pistol handy to control flare-ups, and be careful not to overcook the turkey; the meat should be moist.

Serves 8 people.

VENISON

SMOKED VENISON ROAST

1	venison hindquarter
4-6	strips bacon cut into ½" pieces
1	onion, cut into strips
2	large oranges quartered
2	large grapefruit quartered
1	onion, sliced
	aluminum foil
¼	cup Worcestershire sauce
1	T. seasoned salt
1	T. minced garlic
1¾	cups barbecue sauce
	mesquite wood chips

Heat smoker. Place pan of water under place where hindquarter will be.

Rinse hindquarter; pat dry. Cut slits about 2 inches apart over surface of meat and place bacon pieces and onion pieces inside. Cut a pocket in the center of the side of hindquarter; place oranges, grapefruit and sliced onion in pocket. Place hindquarter on foil. Pour Worcestershire sauce into pocket; rub seasoned salt and garlic on top of hindquarter. Wrap foil around and pour half of barbecue sauce on meat.

Cook roast in smoker for 7 hours. After 6 hours, soak the wood chips in water for 30 minutes, then drain and place in smoker. Let chips smoke for final 30 minutes. Top smoked hindquarter with remaining barbecue sauce and serve it.

Randy Litchfield
Thomaston, Georgia

DEER STEAK AND POTATO SOUP

This is a nice, easy dish for camp or a busy Saturday at home.

2	deer steaks, cubed	1	cup sliced mushrooms
¼	cup flour	2	T. Worcestershire sauce
2	cups potatoes, cubed	1	T. garlic juice
2	cups beef broth	1	package onion soup mix
1½	cups water		

After you have cut up your steak and vegetables. Spray a large slow cooker with non-stick cooking spray. Put the flour in a plastic bag and put your steak cubes in a few at a time to coat them. Then add remaining ingredients to the cooker. Cook at low heat 6 hours, or until the potatoes are tender.

Eugene Taylor
Aliquippa, Pennsylvania

Eugene Taylor

VENISON STROGANOFF

1 lb. ground venison
1 medium onion, chopped
2 T. butter
1 clove garlic, minced
1 tsp. salt
½ tsp. paprika
   pepper to taste
   parsley to taste
1 T. Worcestershire sauce
1 can cream of chicken soup
1 can beef broth
1 cup sour cream

In large skillet or Dutch oven, cook venison, onion, butter, garlic, salt, paprika, pepper and parsley over medium heat until onion is tender. Add 1 tablespoon Worcestershire sauce and cook for 5 minutes stirring constantly. Add soup and broth to venison and simmer for 10 minutes Add sour cream and heat through. Serve over mashed potatoes or noodles.

Don G. Boyer
Sugar Loaf, PA

BACKWOODS MEDICIETTES

This makes a great appetizer.

1   lb. venison steak, cubed
1½ cups Italian dressing
2   cups Italian style bread crumbs

Marinate steak cubes in dressing overnight. Dredge cubes through bread crumbs until well covered. Bake at 375° for 20-30 minutes in baking dish. Serve hot.

Jeff Sager
Lansing, Michigan

VENISON STEAK WITH MUSHROOM GRAVY

2-3 lbs. venison, elk, bear or antelope steaks,
        fat removed
¼   cup white vinegar
      water
2   cans cream of mushroom soup
      salt and pepper to taste
¼-½ cup milk

In a large bowl, combine venison with ¼ cup vinegar and enough water to cover steaks. Let soak for ½ hour to remove blood. Rinse steaks thoroughly; pat dry.

Place steaks in skillet and cover with water. Bring to boil, reduce heat, then simmer, covered, 1½ hours or until fork tender. Pour off water. Add cream of mushroom soup and enough milk to gain desired consistency of gravy. Simmer approximately 30 minutes. Season to taste. Guaranteed to taste better than beef!

James Lilley
Athens, Michigan

LAVERNE'S CANNED VENISON

Cut meat into bite-size pieces and pack into sterile pint jars. To each jar, add ¼ teaspoon salt, ¼-½ teaspoon black pepper and golf-ball-size pieces of ground beef suet. Keep ¾ inch air space at top of each jar.

Place jars in pressure cooker and add 2 quarts water and 2 tablespoon vinegar to pressure cooker. Pressure cook pints at 10 pounds for 75 minutes. Reduce pressure normally. Jars can also be processed by the water-bath method for 3 hours.

Laverne C. Wubben
Hazel Green, Wisconsin

Paul Kesteloot

VENISON OLÉ!

2   lbs. ground venison
2   lbs. processed cheese, cubed
1   can enchilada sauce
1   can chili (without beans)
1   large onion, chopped
½   cup chopped canned jalapeño peppers, drained

Combine cubed cheese, enchilada sauce, and chili in a slow cooker or large deep pot. Cook over low heat until cheese melts, stirring often.

Using a non-stick skillet, brown the venison with onions over medium heat. Add meat and onion mixture to the melted cheese mixture and stir well to mix. Add the jalapeño peppers and stir. Cover and simmer for 1 hour, stirring occasionally. Serve with side dish of tortilla chips.

Paul Kesteloot
Rochester Hills, Michigan

ISLAND TERIYAKI VENISON

This is a recipe my wife, Pam, decided to try. It's easy to make, with very little preparation time, and you won't be able to get it off the grill fast enough at your next barbecue.

1-3 lbs. venison steaks (thin chip steaks)
½ cup brown sugar
2 tsp. salad oil
1 tsp. ginger powder
½ tsp. meat tenderizer
¼ tsp. pepper
2 cloves garlic, chopped

To make marinade, mix all ingredients except venison in large dish. Add venison, marinate at least 6 hours or overnight.

Barbecue over a medium flame, 1-2 minutes on each side depending on the thickness of the steaks.

Jeff Kihlmire
Chinook, Washington

GRILLED VENISON CHOPS

4 butterflied venison chops
barbecue sauce
Worcestershire sauce
ground cloves

salt
pepper
fresh mushrooms, sliced
8 strips thick-cut bacon

Prepare a marinade to taste using barbecue sauce, Worcestershire sauce, cloves and salt and pepper. Marinate chops for ½ hour. Stuff inside of chops with mushrooms. Fold chops around mushrooms and wrap with bacon. Secure with toothpick and grill over medium heat until done, approximately 10-15 minutes.

Rod Brossart
Crystal Lake, Illinois

SIMPLE SALISBURY STEAK

1 lb. ground venison
½ cup bread crumbs
1 egg, beaten
1 medium onion, chopped
1 can cream of mushroom soup
1 can sliced mushrooms, drained

Mix venison, bread crumbs, egg, onion and ⅓ can of soup; shape into 6-8 patties. Brown in skillet and place in baking pan. Mix remaining soup and mushrooms together and pour over patties. Bake at 350° for 30 minutes.

Gary L. Rupert
Avonmore, Pennsylvania

RED BEAN VENISON CHILI

1½ lbs. ground venison
1 large onion, chopped
1 green bell pepper, chopped
1 cup chopped celery
   allspice and chili powder, as desired
7 cups water
2 cans tomato soup
1 large can tomato sauce
1 large can red kidney beans

Brown venison, onion, green pepper, celery, allspice and chili powder. Add remaining ingredients. Bring to a boil, reduce heat and simmer at least 1 hour; or cook in slow cooker on high approximately 1 hour, reduce to low until you're ready to eat. For something different, peel and dice 4-5 potatoes. Boil until tender, drain and add to chili.

Gary L. Rupert
Avonmore, Pennsylvania

JEFF'S UP-NORTH PASTY

¼ lb. venison steak, cubed
1 pkg. ready-made pie crust
1 small onion, chopped
1 medium potato, cubed
1 large carrot, chopped
2 T. butter
  salt and pepper

On a baking sheet tray, lay out pie crust. Pile venison, onion, potato and carrot on one half; put butter on top. Add salt and pepper to taste. Fold crust over and pinch closed. Poke a few small holes in top and bake at 350° for 1-1½ hours.

Jeff Sager
Lansing, Michigan

KENTUCKY VENISON STEW

½ lb. venison meat, cubed
4 cups water
2 large white onions, chopped
6 medium carrots, chopped
5 potatoes, chopped
2 ribs celery, chopped
2 T. garlic powder
1 T. dried oregano
1 T. black pepper
1 T. dried basil
¼ cup soy sauce
¼ cup Worcestershire sauce
1 tsp. hot pepper sauce
  salt to taste
1 cup tomato juice
2 cups chopped tomatoes

Do not soak meat in salt water overnight! Combine meat, water and vegetables in large pot and bring to a boil. Add remaining ingredients, except hot pepper sauce and salt; cover and simmer 30 minutes. Add tomato juice and chopped tomatoes; simmer, uncovered, for 30 minutes.

Clark E. Akers
Robinson Creek, Kentucky

SPICY MEXICAN CASSEROLE

This recipe is low in both fat and cholesterol. However, the cheese and margarine are really the only things changed from my original recipe. The cheese could be changed to a processed cheese, and the lower fat margarine to regular margarine; I sometimes substitute olive oil for the margarine. Fresh green chilies added are a real delight for those who like it hot.

3/4 lb. venison, cut into ½" strips
2 tsp. garlic powder
2 tsp. salt
2 tsp. finely ground black pepper
2 tsp. onion powder
3 T. low fat margarine
2 cups cooked brown rice
1 10-oz. can diced tomatoes and green chilies
1 16-oz. can refried beans
2 cups grated low-fat cheese

Season venison strips with garlic powder, salt, pepper and onion powder (fajita seasoning powder can be used instead of the individual seasonings.) Sauté strips with margarine over medium heat until done.

Add tomatoes and chilies to cooked rice. Place rice in bottom of baking dish sprayed with non-stick cooking spray. Sprinkle with ½ cup of cheese. Place sautéed venison over rice. Layer beans over venison. Add remaining grated cheese on top. Cover with foil or glass lid.

Bake at 350° for 30 minutes or until hot. (It is really important to cover this dish because the cheese has no fat and will dry out; the moisture of the casserole needs to be kept in.)

Lynda Reid
Goldthwaite, Texas

Roy S. Robison, III

ROY'S VENISON CHILI

2   lbs. cubed venison
    steaks
1   large onion, chopped
8   cloves of garlic,
    whole
1   T. vegetable oil
1   quart stewed
    tomatoes
2   small cans tomato
    paste

3   cans Mexican-style
    kidney beans
1   pkg. taco
    seasoning mix
1   T. chili powder
1   tsp. cayenne
    pepper
1   tsp. black pepper
2   dried cayenne
    peppers, whole

In a deep skillet on high heat, brown venison cubes with onion, garlic cloves, and oil. Reduce heat to medium. Add stewed tomatoes, tomato paste, taco seasoning mix, chili powder, cayenne pepper and black pepper. Mix well. Simmer over medium heat for 10 minutes.

Pour mixture into slow cooker. Add beans and dried cayenne peppers. Cook on low for 10-12 hours. Serve with fresh Italian bread.

Roy S. Robison, III
Oxford, Connecticut

DEER STEW

1¹/₂-2 lbs. deer stew meat
    green bell peppers, sliced
    onions, sliced
1 bottle teriyaki sauce

Put meat in slow cooker; add green peppers and onions to taste. Add teriyaki sauce. Cook on medium to high for 4-5 hours. Add salt and pepper or other seasoning if desired. Serve over rice or mashed potatoes. Do not add water or any other liquid; the stew makes its own.

Bruce F. McGowen
Brunswick, Maine

VENISON JERKY DE LA VERA

1 lb. venison cut into strips about 1x5" long and
    ⅛-¼" thick
½ cup Worcestershire sauce
⅓ cup soy sauce
2 T. liquid smoke
1 tsp. seasoned salt
¾ tsp. garlic powder
¾ tsp. onion salt
¼ tsp. pepper

Combine meat and all other ingredients in a plastic bag. Refrigerate overnight, stirring occasionally. Drain liquid from meat and blot meat well with paper towel. Cook 3 hours directly on oven rack at 140°; or if you have the time and patience, insert a toothpick in the end of the meat and hang it between grates on oven rack. Keep oven door cracked so moisture can escape. This is by far the best tasting jerky we have ever had. We're sure everyone will agree once they've tried it.

Christopher and Lisa delaVera
Windsor, New York

STEVE'S EASY GROUND-VENISON JERKY

2	lbs. ground venison	1	tsp. meat tenderizer
2	T. salt	1	tsp. ground cardamom
1½	tsp. seasoning salt	½	tsp. dried marjoram
1	tsp. garlic powder	2	T. liquid smoke
1	tsp. black pepper	2	T. water
1	tsp. cayenne pepper		

Mix venison with spices and refrigerate overnight. Press meat between sheets of wax paper to ⅛ inch thick. Remove top sheet of paper.

Mix liquid smoke and water; brush mixture over meat. Invert flattened meat directly on oven rack; remove paper. Bake at 150° for 3-4 hours until dry, then cut into strips.

Steve Hunter
Greensburg, Indiana

VENISON TRAIL BOLOGNA

2   lbs.ground venison
1   lb. ground spicy pork sausage
¼   cup water
2   T. quick curing salt (such as Morton TenderQuick)
2   tsp. black pepper
1½ tsp. liquid smoke
½   tsp. garlic or onion salt
½   tsp. dry mustard

In bowl, combine all ingredients; mix well. Form mixture into 2 inch diameter rolls about 8 inches long. Wrap rolls in plastic and refrigerate for 24 hours. Remove plastic wrap. Bake rolls at 300° for 1 hour, or until firm.

Bill Wanpler
Lancaster, Ohio

Tom Gaither

VEGETABLE VENISON STEW

1	lb. venison, cubed	1	can green beans, drained
1/2	cup butter	1	can corn, drained
1	onion, chopped	1	can peas, drained
1	cup flour	1	can carrots, drained
2	cans chicken broth	2	cans peeled potatoes, drained
1	can beef broth		salt and pepper to taste

In large pot, melt butter over medium heat. Add venison and onion; cook until meat is browned. Add flour and whisk thoroughly. While whisking, add chicken and beef broth.

Add beans, corn, peas and carrots to pot. Cut up potatoes,

Add to pot, and reduce heat. Simmer for 2 hours over medium heat. Add salt and pepper to taste.

Tom Gaither
Minier, Illinois

GREEN CHILI ENCHILADAS

These are quick and easy and so good. The original recipe was given to me by a friend and I adapted it for venison and to a lower fat version. Canned green chilies may be used, but I use the fresh ones when they are available. The New Mexico Chilies are the best.

1	lb. ground venison
3	cloves garlic, minced
1	T. canola or olive oil
1	can green chili enchilada sauce
4-5	green chilies, chopped
1	tsp. dried oregano
1	tsp. ground cumin
1/2	tsp. dried cilantro (coriander leaves)
6	corn tortillas
1	onion, chopped
1½	cups grated low-fat cheese

In skillet, cook venison, garlic and oil over medium heat until venison is browned; drain any fat. Add enchilada sauce, chilies and seasonings. Simmer to allow flavors to mingle. You are low on liquids, so be careful not to burn. I use a non-stick skillet.

Heat the tortillas, one at a time, in a small amount of oil in a small hot skillet. As you finish heating each tortilla, top it with the meat mixture, onion and cheese. They may be double-stacked. I sometimes put these under the broiler in the oven for a few minutes to melt the cheese on top. A processed cheese may be substituted for the low-fat cheese I use.

Lynda Reid
Goldthwaite, Texas

VENISON SLOPPY JOE

1½   lbs. ground venison
   1   medium onion, chopped
   ½   medium green bell pepper, chopped
   ¼   cup chopped celery
   1   can tomato soup
   ¼   cup ketchup
   ¼   cup barbecue sauce
       salt and pepper to taste

Brown venison burger, onion, bell pepper and celery in skillet over medium heat. Drain; add remaining ingredients. Simmer for 2 hours, stirring occasionally.

Bill Wanpler
Lancaster, Ohio

BARBECUED BEANS WITH VENISON BURGER

   1   lb. ground venison, deer or elk
   1   medium onion, chopped
   1   T. vegetable oil
   1   large can baked beans
   ½   cup ketchup
   2   T. apple cider vinegar
   1   T. Worcestershire sauce
   ½   tsp. hot pepper sauce
   ½   tsp. salt
   ¼   tsp. pepper

Preheat oven to 350° F. Brown venison and onion in skillet with oil. Blend all ingredients together in 2-quart casserole. Bake in preheated oven for 45 minutes.

Al Salz
Rome, Illinois

WILD GAME SPREAD

1 lb. cooked venison meat	1 tsp. horseradish
½ cup chili sauce	salt and pepper
½ cup mayonnaise	to taste

Grind meat, using a coarse plate on an electric or hand grinder. Add the rest of the ingredients to the meat and mix well. (More or less mayonnaise may be used to taste.) Serve as sandwich spread on bread or as an appetizer with crackers.

Danny Hudson
Millwood, Kentucky

CHICKEN FRIED BACKSTRAP

venison backstrap	flour
buttery crackers	eggs, beaten
dried oregano	olive oil
cracked black pepper	1 cup milk

For coating, place crackers in a plastic bag and crush with a rolling pin until fine; add a generous dash of oregano and cracked black pepper, and mix well. Cut backstrap into ¼ inch-thick steaks; pound with meat mallet. Set steaks aside on paper towels to dry.

In three separate bowls, put out flour, beaten eggs and coating mix. Dip steaks in flour, then egg, coating mix. Set steaks aside for at least 20 minutes, to allow the egg to set up.

Heat olive oil in frying pan over medium heat until hot. Fry steaks until coating is brown; turn over and repeat. Drain on paper towels.

For gravy, drain all but 1 tablespoon of pan drippings, add 1 tablespoon flour, and stir to mix. Add 1 cup milk, and cook until thickened, stirring constantly. I like to add a little sugar and pepper to the gravy. This recipe will serve as many as you like depending on the amount of backstrap you use. Serve with mashed potatoes and a green salad.

John Lopez
Galveston, Texas

CABIN VENISON PIE

My family and friends give this recipe rave reviews whenever it's served. The beauty of this recipe is its simplicity. It is a good hearty meal that's sure to take the wrinkles out of the hungriest companion.

1 lb. ground venison
1 large onion, diced
1 can beef with vegetable soup
1 pie shell
6 medium potatoes, cooked and mashed

Brown venison in skillet over medium heat. Move meat to one side of the skillet, add onion and sauté until onion is tender. Add soup to the skillet with the venison and onion. Mix thoroughly.

Reduce the heat under the skillet allowing the soup mixture to heat through while lining a 3 inch-deep casserole dish with the pie shell. Fill shell with skillet mixture. Top with the prepared mashed potatoes. Bake in oven at 350° for 50 minutes, or until top of potatoes is a golden brown. Serve immediately.

Norman E Rose
Alexandria, Virginia

RICK'S SWISS VENISON STEAK SANDWICHES

3 lbs. venison tenderloin
4 green bell peppers, sliced
8 oz. fresh mushrooms, sliced
2 cans spaghetti sauce
1 T. pepper
1 T. garlic salt
1 cup margarine or butter, divided
kaiser or hoagie rolls

Cut the tenderloin into ⅛-¼ inch thick steaks; do not butterfly. Brown the steaks in a frying pan with butter or margarine until done. Sauté the pepper and mushrooms in separate fry pans in butter. Place all ingredients except rolls, in a slow cooker; cook for 5-8 hours. Serve mixture on rolls. Be very careful; this recipe is addicting.

Eric R. Blachek
Hallstead, Pennsylvania

Paul Squazzo

VENISON CUTLET PARMESAN

venison steaks, cut ¼" thick
2   eggs
1   cup milk
3   cups Italian bread crumbs
1   jar spaghetti sauce
    Parmesean cheese, grated
    mozzarella cheese, grated

Beat eggs and milk together. Dip steaks in mixture. Coat meat with seasoned Italian bread crumbs. Brown steaks in skillet.

Cover bottom of baking pan with thin layer of spaghetti sauce. Place meat on sauce. Top the meat with remaining sauce. Sprinkle with Parmesan cheese and generous amount of mozzarella cheese. Cover with aluminum foil. Bake at 350° for 30-45 minutes.

Paul Squazzo
Pensacola, Florida

VENISON TENDERLOIN IN APPLE-CRANBERRY SAUCE

1 lb. tenderloin, sliced into medallions ¼" thick
½ tsp. dried thyme
¼ tsp. salt
¼ tsp. black pepper (fresh ground)
1 cup onion, chopped
2 tsp. canola oil
2 large tart apples, peeled, cored and thinly sliced.
1 16 oz. can whole cranberry sauce
1 T. Worcestershire sauce
1 T. apple cider vinegar
2 T. packed brown sugar
8 oz. uncooked egg noodles

Sprinkle venison with thyme, salt, pepper. Place meat, onion and canola oil in Dutch oven. Cook over medium heat, stirring frequently, until meat is no longer pink. Add apples, cranberry sauce, Worcestershire, vinegar and brown sugar. Stir to mix well.

Bring to boil. Reduce heat, cover and simmer for 40 minutes. Stir occasionally till tender. To serve, pour over 8 oz. egg noodles, cooked according to package directions.

Mark E. Wilcox
Kingston, Illinois

BARBECUE SAUCE

1 cup soy sauce
1 tsp. ginger powder
1 tsp. dry mustard
1 tsp. meat tenderizer
3-6 whole cloves
3 cloves garlic, minced

Mix and pour over grilled steak.

Emanuel E. Yoder
Baltic, Ohio

DALLAS' VENISON ROAST

venison roast	vegetable shortening
garlic salt	baby potatoes
poultry seasoning	baby carrots
black pepper	sliced onion
flour	

Rub the meat with garlic salt, poultry seasoning and black pepper to taste; then coat with flour. Melt shortening over medium-high heat in roaster or plain skillet. Add roast and brown all sides to seal in juices.

Place roast on a rack in a covered roaster or heavy kettle and bake at 350° for 1 hour. Surround roast with vegetables and bake 1 hour more. Make gravy with the remaining juices and serve with a cool glass of white wine.

Dallas Knutson
Hubbard, Iowa

WINE-ROASTED VENISON LEG

1	venison hindquarter	2	T. minced garlic
5	lb. potatoes, peeled	1	T. black pepper
5	lb. carrots, peeled	1	tsp. cayenne pepper
3	large onions, sliced	1	tsp. dried rosemary
6	ribs celery, chopped	1	tsp. dried thyme
	into 3" lengths	1/2	gallon red wine
1	T. salt	6-8	strips bacon
3/4	cup brown sugar		
1/4	cup snipped fresh parsley		

Place venison leg in large roasting pan. Place whole potatoes and carrots in roasting pan around leg. Place onion rings and celery in roasting pan around leg.

Mix all brown sugar, herbs and spices in a separate mixing bowl. When blended well, sprinkle over contents of roasting pan. Lay strips of bacon across venison leg. Add wine to roasting pan. Bake at 350° for 3-4 hours depending on the size of the leg. Happy hunting!!!

Ron Campano
West Sand Lake, New York

Chad Turky

VENISON POT ROAST

3-4 lb. venison shoulder, rump or round roast
    all-purpose flour
    salt and pepper
½ cup water
5 whole carrots
5 whole potatoes
5 whole onions
    turnips or celery, if desired

Dredge meat in flour; add salt and pepper and brown in melted shortening in Dutch oven over medium-high heat. Add water, reduce heat and cover.

Braise the meat for 2-3 hours. When meat is tender, add the vegetables. Add more hot water if necessary and cook until vegetables are tender. Make a gravy of the liquid in the pan and pour over meat and vegetables.

Chad Turky
North Little Rock, Arkansas

PEPPER STEAK

1½ lbs. of venison steaks ¾" thick
¼ cup seasoned flour
2 T. shortening
1 can tomato soup
½ cup water
1 green bell pepper, cut into 8 strips
1 medium onion, minced or sliced
4 thin slices lemon
1 clove of garlic, minced
1 T. lemon juice

Cover steak with seasoned flour. Brown steaks on both sides in shortening in skillet over medium heat. Add remaining ingredients. Cover and cook over low heat for 45 minutes or until steak is tender.

Bill Wunpler
Lancaster, Ohio

WILD GAME BARBECUE GLAZE

3 cups ketchup
1 cup clover honey
½ cup liquid smoke
½ tsp. sage

Combine all ingredients. Cook over low heat to thicken if desired. Makes enough glaze for 6 steaks.

Dewey Simpson Jr.
Ritzville, Washington

HAL'S CHILI

3½	lb. venison or elk roast, cubed	1	tsp. crushed red pepper
3	T. oil	2	cups beef broth
2	cups chopped onion	1	large can whole tomatoes
4	cloves garlic, minced	1	can tomato paste
¼	cup chili powder	1	T. salt
1½	tsp. diced oregano	1	tsp. sugar
1½	tsp. ground cumin	1-2	T. cornmeal, to thicken

Heat 3 tablespoon of oil in large heavy pot. Add meat; sear, turning constantly, for 3-4 minutes until meat is browned. Add onion and garlic; sauté until onion is wilted but not browned.

Stir in chili powder, oregano, cumin and crushed red pepper; mix well until onion is coated. Add beef broth, tomatoes, tomato paste, salt and sugar. Mix well, breaking up tomatoes. Cover and simmer for 1 hour. Uncover and simmer an additional 1 hour. If chili is too thin, add cornmeal and stir.

Richard Morton
Myrtle Creek, Oregon

GROUND VENISON JERKY

4	lbs. ground venison
4	T. seasoned salt
2	T. tenderizer
2-3	T. liquid smoke
2	tsp. ground black pepper

Mix all ingredients together until tacky. Line 2-3 jelly roll pans with foil. Spread meat onto pans and flatten to ⅟₁₆ inch thick. Freeze for at least 3 hours. Remove frozen meat from pans and cut into 1 inch-wide strips. Place on oven racks and bake at 200° for 2 hours for chewy jerky or 3 hours for a dry, hard jerky. You may want to check often after 2 hours of baking to achieve desired doneness.

Darrell Berreth
Hecla, South Dakota

SHEPHERD'S PIE

  2 lbs. ground venison
6-7 potatoes, peeled
  1/4 tsp. salt
     dash of pepper
  2 T. milk
  1 T. butter
  1 can yellow corn

Brown venison and set aside. Cook potatoes and mash, using milk, butter, salt and pepper.

Put venison in bottom of a 2-quart casserole dish. Drain corn and spread over venison. Top off with the mashed potatoes. Bake at 350° about 45 minutes or until potatoes develop a crunchy brown crust.

Fred Archer
Balto, Maryland

MAINE CHILI

  2 lbs. ground venison
  1 tsp. olive oil
  2 medium onions, chopped
  1 16-oz. can light red kidney beans
  1 16-oz. can dark red kidney beans
  2 28-oz. cans whole tomatoes
  1 6-oz. can tomato paste
  1 T. chili powder
  1/4 tsp. cayenne pepper
     salt to taste

Brown venison in olive oil. Add onions and pepper; sauté until tender. Mix remaining ingredients with venison, onion and pepper in a large pot and simmer 1-2 hours, stirring occasionally.

Fred Archer
Balto, Maryland

VENISON TACO PIE

1 lb. ground venison
1 medium onion, chopped
1 package taco seasoning mix
1 8-oz. can tomato sauce
1 cup crushed chips

1 cup sour cream
1 8-oz. can refrigerated
    crescent dinner rolls
2 cups shredded cheddar
    cheese

Heat oven to 350°. Brown venison and onion in large skillet. Stir in taco seasoning and tomato sauce; mix well.

Unroll crescent roll dough; press onto bottom and sides of 9 inch pie pan to form crust. Press to seal perforations. Sprinkle crust with ¾ cup crushed chips. Spread venison mixture over chips and bake for 15 minutes

Add sour cream, then cheese and top with remaining chips. Bake additional 15 minutes or until crust is brown.

Lowell Henline Jr.
Wyoming, Michigan

HENLINE'S HUNTER'S CHILI

4 lbs. ground venison
2 T. bacon fat
3 medium onions,
    chopped
3 green bell peppers,
    chopped
1 stalk celery, chopped
2-3 cloves garlic, minced

1 28-oz. can whole
    tomatoes
2 T. parsley flakes
2 T. chili powder
    salt and pepper to taste
1 can ranch style
    beans

In Dutch oven, brown meat; remove from heat and set aside. In large skillet, melt bacon fat; cook and stir onions, green peppers, celery, and garlic until tender.

Add vegetables and all remaining ingredients, except beans, to meat in Dutch oven. Heat to boiling, reduce heat and cover. Simmer for 1 hour. Stir in beans and cook uncovered for 30 minutes.

Lowell E. Henline Jr.
Wyoming, Michigan

Greg Hall

DEER DIPS

1 lb. ground venison
1 pkg. dry onion soup mix
  dash seasoning salt
  dash black pepper
1 pkg. au jus mix
8 slices swiss cheese
8 slices bacon, fried

Mix venison, onion soup, salt and pepper together. Form thick oblong patties and barbecue or fry until done.

Heat au jus in a saucepan according to package directions. Place cheese on cooked burgers, allowing it to melt; add 2 strips bacon. Place patties on rolls and dip in au jus.

Greg Hall
Marysville, Washington

WISCONSIN VENISON AND MACARONI STEW

1 lb. ground venison
1 cup onion, chopped
3/4 cup uncooked macaroni
3 cups potatoes, cut in
   1/2" cubes
3 medium carrots, sliced
1 can diced tomatoes
1 8-oz. can tomato sauce
1 cup ketchup
1 cup water

1 T. brown sugar
1 1/2 tsp. chili powder
1 tsp. Worcestershire
   Sauce
1 tsp. seasoned salt
1 tsp. salt
1 tsp. dried oregano
1 tsp. lemon juice
1/4 tsp. pepper

Brown venison with onion. Cook macaroni and drain. Combine all ingredients in large pot and let simmer for approximately 1 hour. Serve immediately or allow to cool overnight, then heat and serve. As with most recipes of this kind, it will taste best the next day or two.

Bernard Lawrence
Pardeeville, Wisconsin

VENISON ROUND STEAK

2 lbs. venison round steak
1 tsp. salt
1/4 tsp. pepper
1 tsp. garlic powder
1/2-1 tsp. fennel seed

2-3 T. olive oil
1 cup flour
1 small onion sliced
2 carrots, sliced
3-4 potatoes, cubed

Cut round steak into serving size pieces. Season both sides of meat with salt, pepper, garlic powder, fennel and coat with flour.

Brown both sides of meat in olive oil. Add 1/2 cup of water and simmer for 1/2 hour; add onion, carrots and potatoes. Continue cooking until vegetables are tender, adding water as needed.

John and Gloria Curran
Dayton, Nevada

RITA'S EASY SLOW-COOKER VENISON ROAST

1	3-5 lb. venison roast, boned	1	medium onion, sliced
	salt		
	pepper	1/2	cup brown sugar
	garlic powder	1/4	tsp. seasoned salt
1	can beer	1/4	tsp. dry basil
1 1/3	cups ketsup		

Season roast to taste with salt, pepper and garlic powder. (Don't brown meat.) Place roast in slow cooker. Combine remaining ingredients and pour over roast. Cook on high for 5 hours and then 5 more hours on low, or until tender.

Edward Hollister
Andover, New Jersey

VENISON ITALIAN SAUSAGE

20	lbs. venison
20	lbs. Boston pork butts
1 1/2	lbs. Parmesan or romano cheese, grated
4	large cans tomatoes
3	bunches fresh parsley, chopped
2	cups fennel seed
6	T. cracked black pepper

Cut venison and pork into about 1 inch cubes. Mix remaining ingredients together and pour on the meat. Mix thoroughly.

Grind mixture through 3/8 inch grinder plate. Mix again; then grind through 3/16 inch grinder plate. Stuff mixture into hog casings, about 1 inch in diameter; tie casings at about 6 inch intervals. You can also leave the sausage in bulk for patties.

Ken Ebert
Arnold, Missouri

Kevin J. Graves

GRAVES' PEPPERED VENISON JERKY

3-4 lbs. venison meat
2 T. liquid smoke
1 cup soy sauce
1 cup teriyaki sauce
2 T. ground black pepper
2 T. meat tenderizer
2 T. chili powder
2 T. seasoned salt
2 T. onion salt
2 T. garlic powder
2 T. dried oregano
4 T. coarse ground black pepper, divided

Slice venison into strips about ⅛ inch thick and set aside. Mix all other ingredients except 2 tablespoons coarse pepper in a large bowl and stir well. Add meat and stir. Marinate, covered, overnight in the refrigerator.

Lay the meat in a single layer on food dehydrator racks and sprinkle with remaining pepper. Dry for up to 14 hours until dry and chewy to individual taste. Jerky should be leathery but still flexible when done. Makes 40-50 jerky strips.

Kevin J. Graves
Hampton, Virginia

BARBECUE VENISON

I have tried all the fancy recipes and watched the videos. They are time-consuming, and they give the cook something to talk about. Here is the best and simplest way.

Take a venison roast out of the freezer and put it in the slow cooker in the morning. Cook it late into the evening. Unplug the slow cooker, pour in enough of your favorite barbecue sauce to cover the roast. Refrigerate overnight.

The next day, invite your friends for dinner and plug the slow cooker in to heat the roast. You don't need anything else. The hardest part will be knowing what to serve with it. The secret is to let the meat sit one day in the barbecue sauce.

Donald A. Vinegar
La Crosse, Wisconsin

SLUM GULLIGAN

1½	lbs. ground venison	1	medium yellow onion, chopped
16	oz. uncooked elbow macaroni	½	tsp. olive oil
2	cans whole tomatoes	1	8-oz. jar processed cheese spread
1	green bell pepper, chopped	1	tsp. salt
1	red bell pepper, chopped	½	tsp. pepper

Cook macaroni until tender. Drain and add cheese spread. Set aside.

Sauté peppers and onion in olive oil. Add venison; mix in tomatoes, salt and pepper. Simmer for 15 minutes Remove from heat and add macaroni and cheese. Blend together and serve.

Fred Archer
Baltimore, Maryland

RAGOUT OF VENISON

Marinade:
4¼ cups red wine vinegar, divided
½ tsp. dried marjoram
4 juniper berries, crushed
1 bay leaf
1 tsp. dried rosemary
2 whole cloves
¼ tsp. dried thyme
10 peppercorns
1 cup coarsely chopped celery
1 cup thinly sliced carrots
1 cup quartered small onions
2 sprigs parsley
salt to taste

In a saucepan, combine ¼ cup red wine vinegar, the marjoram, juniper berries, bay leaf, rosemary, cloves, thyme and peppercorns. Bring to a boil and simmer for 5 minutes. Empty the mixture into a bowl and add the remaining ingredients. Makes 2 quarts of marinade.

Ragout:
1 5-lb. venison shoulder cut into 2" cubes
2 qts. marinade (recipe above)
¼ cup peanut oil
¼ cup flour
salt and pepper
¼ cup currant jelly
⅓ lb. lean salt pork
10 white pearl onions
1 tsp. butter
1 tsp. sugar
3 cups sliced mushrooms

Place venison pieces in marinade, cover with foil and refrigerate for 2-3 days, no longer.

Preheat oven to 400°. Remove the meat from the marinade and set it aside. Drain the vegetables, reserving the solids and the liquid. Heat 2 tablespoons oil in 1-2 medium skillets. Brown the meat, transferring to an oven-proof kettle as you are browning it. Use more oil if necessary, but don't go overboard. Add a little more oil to another skillet and cook the reserved solids over high heat for about 5 minutes Add this to the meat. Sprinkle the flour over all and stir. Cook for about 3 minutes, then add the reserved liquid. Add salt and pepper to taste. Bring to a boil and cover. Place the kettle in the oven and bake for 2 hours.

Remove from the oven, tilt the kettle and skim off excess fat from the surface. Add the jelly and stir until dissolved. Simmer for 5 minutes. Cut the salt pork into small strips, place in a sauce pan, cover with water and bring to a boil. Simmer for 1 minute and drain.

Peel the onions and combine them in a saucepan with water to barely cover. Add the butter and sugar and a dash of salt. Cook until the liquid evaporates and the onions start to take on a brown glaze.

Heat a skillet and add salt pork strips. When crisp, remove, draining well. Add the mushrooms to the salt pork fat. Sprinkle with salt and pepper. Cook for approx. 10 minutes, stirring as needed. Drain well and set aside. Put the onions in a skillet, add the salt pork and mushrooms and cook for about 5 minutes. Sprinkle this mixture over the venison and cook for about 10 minutes.

Lee Prescott
Dolores, Colorado

KEN'S TEXAS STEW

2   lbs. venison roast, cubed
6   carrots, sliced
1   onion, chopped
1   cup chopped celery
1   small can mushrooms drained
1   small can whole tomatoes
$\frac{1}{4}$ tsp. chili powder
$\frac{1}{8}$ tsp. pepper
$\frac{1}{8}$ tsp. ground cumin
$\frac{1}{8}$ tsp. dried rosemary
$\frac{1}{8}$ tsp. dried thyme
$\frac{1}{8}$ tsp. dried marjoram
     salt to taste
2   slices bread, cubed
1   10-oz. package frozen green beans
1   cup red wine

Combine all ingredients except for beans and wine in a Dutch oven; mix well. Bake at 250° for 3 hours Add water if necessary to keep moist. Add beans and wine; bake 30 minutes longer.

You can cook this over an open fire, but the stew will be more tender and tasty if baked. If you cook over a fire you will need to stir occasionally to keep it from burning.

Kenneth Pyka
Pattison, Texas

Chris Wood

BRENDA'S VENISON BARBECUE

3-4 lb. venison roast
½ cup ketchup
¼ cup margarine
¼ cup mustard
2 T. vinegar
2 T. brown sugar
2 T. Worcestershire sauce
½ tsp. hot pepper sauce
¼ tsp. salt

Cook the roast in a slow cooker until well done, then shred. Mix remaining ingredients in a saucepan and bring to a boil. Reduce the heat and let it simmer for 20-30 minutes. Pour over the shredded venison and mix well.

Chris Wood
Laurel, Maryland

VENISON KABOBS TEXAS STYLE

venison meat, cut into 1- 1¹/₂" chunks
smokey barbecue sauce
sliced jalapeño peppers
bacon slices
12" long bamboo skewers

First, pour the barbecue sauce over the venison chunks and mix well. Take one piece of venison and skewer it about four inches down from the point; add one slice of jalapeño pepper, then another piece of venison, a pepper and a third piece of venison. Skewer strip of bacon about ½ inch from its end and wrap around meat and peppers. When you get to the end of the kabob, wrap bacon around the skewer then back to where you started pulling the bacon over the tip of the skewer to hold it in place.

Slide this kabob you just made to the bottom of the skewer and then start another one at the tip as before. This way you will get two kabobs per skewer; by cutting the sticks in two, you make them easier to handle and they won't take up as much room on the grill. The bacon will pull tight around the kabob when done and makes an eye-appealing, mouth-watering morsel

You can also use this recipe for quail and dove. I like to alternate breast halves of quail and dove. It's better to cook these well done and off to the side, not directly above the coals.

Walter M. Ellison
Dallas, Texas

SWEET-N-SOUR MEATBALLS

Here it is! The easiest, best-tasting, never-fail, crowd-pleasing recipe for sweet and sour meatballs. The bread holds the leanest game burger together while the sweet/sour tomato-based sauce cuts any wild taste that may be present. I've even used late-season buck burger in this recipe and the flavor is fabulous.

1½ lbs. ground venison
4 slices crumbled bread or equivalent crushed crackers
salt, pepper, minced onion and garlic, to taste
¼ cup milk
1 egg
2 cups ketchup
1 cup sugar
⅔ cup vinegar
⅔ cup water
2 T. liquid smoke
dash Worcestershire sauce

Mix venison, bread, milk, egg and seasonings together; form mixture into golf-ball-size balls. Place a single layer in a large baking pan. Mix remaining ingredients in bowl and pour over meatballs. Cook, uncovered, at 350° for 50 minutes. Serve with rice or noodles.

Chieko Bowles
Great Falls, Montana

MIKE'S JERKY MARINADE

1 venison hindquarter
4 cups apple cider vinegar
2 cups packed brown
   sugar
1 cup water
2/3 cup lemon pepper
   marinade sauce
1/2 cup apple juice
1/2 cup teriyaki sauce
2 T. hot teriyaki sauce
1/4 cup Worcestershire
   sauce
1/4 cup soy sauce
1/4 cup crushed hot
   chilies
1/4 cup lemon-pepper
   seasoning salt
1/4 cup ground black pepper
1/4 cup szechwan style pepper blend
1/4 cup seasoned pepper blend
2 T. liquid smoke
1/2 tsp. salt
1/2 tsp. ground jalapeño

Michael Aud

Cut meat into thin strips. In large bowl, combine remaining ingredients. Add meat strips; stir. Marinate 24-48 hours in refrigerator.

Drain marinade from strips. Put in dehydrator for 8-10 hours, until jerky is dry but flexible.

Michael Aud
California, Maryland

VENISON STEAK KATHLEEN

This recipe is great with all venison, including deer, elk, moose and caribou, and can be used with various other game, especially upland birds.

venison steaks
1/2 cup Dijon mustard
2 T. honey
1 T. Worcestershire sauce
1-2 tsp. white wine (to taste)
1 tsp. beer (makes nice variation)
1 tsp. red wine vinegar
pepper to taste
garlic powder (if you'd like)

Prepare the marinade/sauce by mixing all ingredients except venison. Spread marinade on venison steaks being sure to cover both sides. Refrigerate 3-4 hours.

Place a small amount of butter in a fry pan, or spray pan with cooking spray; heat pan to medium-high. Sauté steaks to medium well. Do not overcook.

This recipe can also be used to cook game on the barbecue. Extra marinade can be used to baste while grilling. Serve steaks with caramelized onions, carrots and baked potatoes. A hearty wheat or sourdough bread makes a nice complement!

Robert P. Dwyer
Milford, Massachusetts

SWEET AND SOUR VENISON ROAST

1	2½-lb. venison roast	1	onion, sliced
1½	cups vinegar	¼	cup flour
1½	cups water	3	T. shortening
3	bay leaves	1	cup sour cream
1½	tsp. salt	5	ginger snaps, crumbled
½	tsp. pepper		

Place venison in shallow glass dish. Mix vinegar and water and pour over venison. Add bay leaves, salt, pepper and onion. Cover and refrigerate 12-24 hours, turning roast occasionally.

Remove venison from marinade; dry on paper towels. Coat roast with flour and brown in hot shortening in 4-quart pressure cooker. Strain marinade and add 1¼ cups to cooker. Cover and place control on lid. After control jiggles, let cook for 20 minutes. Take cooker from heat. Let cool for 5 minutes, then run cold water over top of the cooker. Test control to be sure pressure has dropped before opening. Stir in sour cream and ginger snap crumbs; heat through.

Kenneth Wright
Caneyville, Kentucky

SALAMI

5	lbs. ground venison
5	tsp. meat tenderizer
5½	tsp. mustard seed
4	tsp. course ground black pepper
2½	tsp. garlic salt
2½	tsp. hickory smoked salt or Salt Plus
2½	tsp. liquid smoke

Mix all ingredients well and refrigerate. Mix well each day for three days. On fourth day, mix one last time and shape mixture into small rolls. Bake at 160° for 8 hours or until rolls form own skin.

Robert R. Lynn
Jasonville, Indiana

STONYMAN DEERLOAF

1¼   lbs. ground venison
  1   egg
  1   onion, diced
  1   tsp. salt
  1   tsp. pepper
  1   tsp. sugar
  ½   cup ketchup
  2   T. steak sauce

Combine all ingredients; mix well. Shape mixture into loaf; place in glass baking dish. Bake at 350° until brown and firm.

Mary Caton
Luray, Virginia

WISCONSIN VENISON STEAKS

6-8   venison steaks
      flour
      seasoned salt
  1   large onion, sliced
  1   cup beer
½-1   cup barbecue sauce (optional)
      mushrooms

Dip steaks in flour and season with salt. Brown in large skillet with onion slices. Add beer and simmer 10-15 minutes. Add barbecue sauce, if desired. Place contents of skillet in roaster and add mushrooms. Bake at 275° for 1½ hours

Al Jenewein
North Freedom, Wisconsin

TWENTY-MINUTE VENISON STEW

1-1½ lbs. venison round steak
   2 T. olive oil
   2 green bell peppers, cleaned and cut into 1" squares
   3 T. red table wine
   2 medium tomatoes, peeled and quartered
   1 tsp. garlic salt
   1 tsp. pepper
   1 can beef gravy

Cut meat ¼ inch thick and into 1½ inch pieces. Heat Dutch oven over very high heat. Add oil, coating sides and bottom of pan; pour out excess. Add meat, peppers, wine, salt and pepper. Stir rapidly and constantly for about 5 minutes, then reduce heat to simmer for 10 minutes. Add tomatoes and gravy. Serve at once over white rice or wild rice.

Al Jenewein
North Freedom, Wisconsin

SLOPPY JOE VENISON MEATLOAF

1½ lbs. ground venison   ½ tsp. salt
  1 cup soft fresh bread   ¼ tsp. pepper
     crumbs   1 can sloppy joe sauce
 ⅓ cup finely chopped onion   1 T. prepared mustard
  1 egg

In a bowl, mix the first 6 ingredients with ½ cup sloppy joe sauce. Shape into loaf and place in shallow baking pan. Bake at 350° for 40 minutes. Drain. Spread mustard over loaf and pour remaining sloppy joe sauce over all. Bake an additional 30 minutes. The mustard kills the wild taste; if you like the wild taste, you may omit the mustard.

Jack Barnes
Dallas, Texas

James Hemp

VIRGINIA VENISON JERKY

venison roast, cut into thin strips
½ cup Worcestershire sauce
¼ cup soy sauce
2 tsp. salt
1 tsp. sugar
1 tsp. meat tenderizer
½ tsp. liquid smoke
½ tsp. pepper

Combine all ingredients in large bowl; mix well. Make sure there is enough liquid to cover meat. Refrigerate overnight, drain and arrange strips in food dehydrator. Cook 10-12 hours.

James Hemp
Staunton, Virginia

Oven Barbecued Swiss Steak

2   lbs. venison round steak cut into 1" thick strips
⅓   cup flour
1   tsp. salt
½   tsp. pepper
¼   tsp. each dried rosemary, oregano, parsley, cilantro
     or your favorite seasonings
     shortening
2   cups seasoned tomatoes
1   T. sugar
1   T. vinegar
     Worcestershire sauce to taste
1   medium to large onion, sliced

Combine flour, salt, pepper and seasonings; coat meat with this mixture. In Dutch oven, brown meat slowly on both sides in hot shortening. Drain off any excess fat.

Combine tomatoes, sugar, vinegar and Worcestershire sauce; pour over meat. Simmer 5 minutes Add onion. Cover and bake at 350° for 1½ hours or until meat is tender.

I suggest some homemade cornbread and perhaps steamed broccoli with this dish. I guarantee you'll be back for more. My wife, who is not a big venison eater, said it was very good!

Dennis Riesterer
Pittsford, Vermont

SUPER BOWL SUNDAY BARBECUE

Socorro's rules for wild game
1. Cool it fast — keep it clean.
2. Soak meat in enough water to completely cover it in the refrigerator for 12-24 hours

      venison, elk, antelope or other game meat, enough for the size crowd you expect to feed
½ large onion sliced
    juice of 1 large lime
¼ cup tarragon red wine vinegar or plain red wine vinegar
1 T. garlic powder
½ tsp. black pepper
½ tsp. dried basil
½ tsp. dried parsley
¼ tsp. dried sage
1 T. light soy sauce

Mix all ingredients, except venison, to make marinade. Drain off initial soaking water. Add fresh water to cover the meat again, then add marinade. Cover and marinate in refrigerator 12 hours or overnight.

Remove the meat from the marinade and place in slow cooker. Add 1 cup water or beef broth, more if needed. If you are using extremely lean meat, add 1 tablespoon olive oil. Cook on low heat until meat is tender enough to shred with a fork, 8-12 hours, depending on your slow cooker and the amount of meat you are using. Remove the meat from the pot and shred into bite-size pieces. Place in a large baking dish.

Sauce: (This is the easy part.) Pour your favorite barbecue sauce over meat and stir to coat evenly. Cover with foil and refrigerate until ready to heat. (Note: It can be used right away, but if you refrigerate it for a couple of hours the meat will pick up more of the barbecue flavor.) To heat, place in a 350° oven for 30 minutes or until the sauce is bubbling. Serve with all your favorite side dishes.

Socorro Heft
Sonora, Texas

Peppery Venison Jerky

8-10 lbs. venison (preferably roast)
¼-⅓ cup Worcestershire sauce
 ¾ cup soy sauce
1¾ cup barbecue sauce
 ½ cup liquid smoke
 ¼ cup steak sauce
 ¼ cup hot pepper sauce
  2 tsp. black pepper (or red)
  1 tsp. cayenne pepper (optional)
  1 box of toothpicks (if using oven)

Cut venison into ⅛ to ¼ inch-thick strips; cut with the grain of the meat. Mix remaining ingredients in a large mixing bowl. Salt can be added to suit taste. Place meat in the sauce and let soak for 12-24 hours in refrigerator.

If using an oven, preheat to 120° or low setting. Drain liquid from venison strips. Place toothpicks in one end of strips and hang on oven racks. Bake for 4-6 hours, or until the jerky is leathery. Leaving a crack in the oven door may help moisture escape. Allow jerky to cool and harden. Take out toothpicks and enjoy.

If using a dehydrator, place strips on the racks and leave for 6-8 hours, or until leathery. Allow to cool. Keep in mind that thicker cuts will take longer to dry.

Robert Fout
Berea, Kentucky

JESS'S NEXT-STEP VENISON CHILI

1   lb. ground venison burger

2   15-oz. cans hot chili beans

1   15-oz. can tomato sauce

1½ cups water (more or less depending on consistency preference)

2   T. ketchup

2   T. brown sugar

1   T. dried onions (fresh is best; may use ¼ cup chopped onions)

2   tsp. hot chili powder

½ tsp. seasoned salt

½ tsp. vinegar

½ tsp. garlic powder (fresh is best; may use 1 T. minced fresh garlic)

½ tsp. Cajun seasoning (can be bought in most grocery stores; if you don't have this, double the amount of hot chili powder)

½ tsp. cayenne pepper (optional)

¼ tsp. pepper

Brown venison in large pan. Add remaining ingredients and simmer for at least ½ hour. All ingredients can be altered according to personal taste. Serve with a topping of shredded cheddar cheese or just eat plain.

Jess Gilland
Onida, South Dakota

LOU'S VENISON SALSA CHILI

2 lbs. ground venison
2 T. peanut oil
1 T. chopped fresh garlic
1/4 tsp. powdered ginger
1 large onion, chopped
1 cup sliced mushrooms
2 T. sherry
1 large can chili beans
2 small cans whole tomatoes, chopped
3 cups tomato juice
1 3/4 cups salsa, hot or mild
1 T. chili powder

In a large soup kettle, combine oil, garlic and ginger. Cook at medium heat for 30 seconds, then add venison and brown. Add onion, mushrooms and sherry; cook for 3 minutes. Add all other ingredients. Cover and simmer for 1/2 hour or more.

Luel D. Gerard
Saginaw, Michigan

SLUMGULLION

1-2 lbs. ground venison or elk
1 large onion, chopped
1 large can pork and beans
1/4-1/3 cup barbecue sauce
1/4-1/3 cup brown sugar
1-2 T. cider vinegar
salt and pepper to taste

Brown onion and ground meat together in large pot. Add remaining ingredients; simmer until thick, stirring occasionally. Serve in warm flour tortillas for burritos, or over rice. This is even better the next day!

Cole and Dianne Engrave
Mira Loma, California

HONEY DIJON CRUSTED BACKSTRAP

1 venison backstrap with silverskin removed,
   or tenders
   salt and pepper
3 cups honey Dijon mustard or bistro sauce
2 cups crushed cracker or bread crumbs
1/4 cup melted butter
   paprika (optional)

Put cleaned backstrap or tender on sheet pan or baking dish. Season the meat with salt and pepper or your own seasoning. Cover entire backstrap with honey Dijon mustard or bistro sauce. Coat surface of meat with cracker crumbs. Drizzle melted butter on top. If desired, sprinkle paprika on top.

Bake at 350° until meat reaches 130°. Venison is better on the rare side, but it can be done to your own taste. If you use tenders, you may need a smaller quantity of each ingredient. This would make a great addition to a family Christmas dinner, where the hunter can carve something different than the old ham or turkey.

This recipe can be used for other game, like pheasant, rabbit, etc.

Billy Joe Goolsby
Jacksonville, Illinois

VERY TASTY VENISON ROAST

1 3 lb. venison roast
   salt and pepper
4 medium potatoes,
   peeled and diced

3 large carrots, sliced
3 stalks celery, sliced
1 pkg. onion soup mix
1 cup water

Place meat in a large roasting pan. Sprinkle with a little salt and pepper. Top with the potatoes, carrots and celery. Add the onion soup mix over the top on the roast. Pour the water on the top and cover with aluminum foil. Bake at 350° for 1-1$^1/_2$ hours.

James Overton
North Augusta, South Carolina

HUNTER'S STEW

3	lbs. venison or beef, cut into ½-1" pieces
4-6	strips bacon, cut into 1-2" lengths
¼	cup Worcestershire sauce
½	T. garlic salt
2	tsp. black pepper
3	cans golden mushroom soup
3	pkgs. onion soup mix
4	cups water
6-8	lbs. potatoes, cut in half
4	medium onions
4-5	lbs. carrots, cut into 3- 4" lengths
½	cup butter
8	oz. fresh mushrooms, cut in half

Place venison in a large pot or roaster. Spread bacon pieces over the meat. Sprinkle with Worcestershire sauce, garlic salt and pepper. Add golden mushroom soup, onion soup mix and 4 cups of water. Cook over medium heat until it comes to a boil, stirring occasionally.

Add potatoes, onions and carrots. Cook on medium to high heat for 45 minutes to 1 hour, or until potatoes can be penetrated with a fork. Turn heat to low.

In a separate skillet, melt butter, and sauté mushrooms. Add the entire contents of the skillet to the stew pot. Continue to cook on low heat, stirring occasionally, for 30 minutes. Serve with fresh biscuits, toast or a side of rice.

Howard T. Martin
Eay Galle, WI

PICKLED VENISON HEART

venison hearts
1 cup sugar

1 cup white vinegar
1 T. pickling spice

Cook venison hearts until tender; slice into thin slices. Bring sugar and vinegar to a boil and add pickling spice to make brine. Layer sliced onion and venison in a covered container. Cover with brine and refrigerate. Multiply the brine to make a sufficient amount to cover the heart and onions.

Howard T. Martin
Eay Galle, WI

HOT VENISON CHILI

2 lbs. ground venison
1-2 lbs. venison steak, cubed
1 large green bell pepper, chopped
2 onions, chopped
2 cloves garlic, minced
1 tsp. salt
  garlic salt
1 large can tomatoes

1 large can tomato sauce
1 jar salsa
1 cup deer broth or a beef bouillon cube
4 T. chili powder
1/2 tsp. hot pepper flakes
2 T. chili powder
2 cans chili beans

Combine ground venison, steak, green pepper, onions and garlic in large skillet. Cook until the meat is done, using a fork to crumble the ground venison while it is cooking. Meanwhile, add salt and some garlic salt; when meat is done, drain grease from pan.

Add remaining ingredients except beans and cook on low for at least 1 hour. Add chili beans and cook for another half hour. Taste and add whatever you think it needs. You can always add more chili powder or hot pepper flakes or salt until you get the taste you like. Be careful with the hot pepper flakes because the longer it cooks the hotter it will get. Good luck.

Conrad Wear
Rocky Point, NC

FRIED VENISON, SOUTHERN STYLE

1 venison loin, thinly sliced
   vegetable oil
2-3 cups flour
   salt and pepper
   garlic salt (optional)
1 large onion, chopped
   water

Cover bottom of iron frying pan with oil. Coat thinly sliced loin with flour and place in hot cooking oil; add salt, pepper and garlic salt while cooking. (Do not overcook, as this will make venison tough.) Continue to fry pieces of loin in batches, adding cooking oil as needed and setting cooked pieces aside. When last batch of venison is placed in frying pan, add onions.

Leave onions in cooking oil after last batch of venison has been taken out. Add cold water to onions and continue cooking in preparation for making gravy. Dissolve flour in a cup of cold water and add to onions in pan, stirring continuously until gravy is golden brown. (Use enough flour to achieve desired consistency.)

Spread gravy over venison or hot biscuits. Close your eyes and enjoy the bounty of a good hunt.

William R. Bayrer
Pantego, North Carolina

NEIL'S VENISON STROGANOFF

1¹/₂ lbs. venison round steak
     flour
     butter
1 cup onion, chopped
1 6-oz. can mushrooms, drained
1 can beef broth
1 tsp. Worcestershire sauce
1 tsp. soy sauce
     salt to taste
1 cup sour cream

Soak venison in salt water overnight. Remove all fat and tendons; cut meat into ¾ inch strips. Roll strips in flour to coat; brown in butter in large skillet.

Remove meat from skillet. Sauté onion and mushrooms in butter until onion is tender. Add meat, broth, Worcestershire sauce, soy sauce and salt to taste. Cover and simmer 45 minutes to 1 hour. Add sour cream and heat through. Serve over noodles or rice.

Neil Bressler
Donaldson, Pennsylvania

MARINATED VENISON CHOPS

4 venison chops
1 bottle Italian dressing
1 T. bacon grease
     salt and pepper to taste

Place chops in bowl, cover with Italian dressing, and marinate for 6-8 hours in refrigerator. Heat bacon grease in cast iron skillet and sear chops. Place in oven and bake at 300° for 15 minutes, or until done. Salt and pepper to taste. Serve with your choice of potatoes.

Tom Gaither
Minier, Illinois

VENISON SCALLOPS IN MUSTARD CREAM SAUCE

1½ lbs. venison scallops (8 very large or 10-12 smaller), pounded
4 T. sweet butter
2 T. vegetable oil
3 green onions, chopped
    salt and freshly ground black pepper, to taste
⅓ cup dry white wine
⅓ cup Dijon mustard (avoid ballpark type mustards)
½ cup crème fraîche or heavy cream
1 large firm ripe tomato, peeled, seeded and chopped

Melt the butter and oil together in a large skillet over medium heat. Add the green onions and cook over low heat for 5 minutes without browning. Raise the heat, add the venison scallops and season to taste with salt and pepper. Cook scallops 1 minute per side; do not overcook and don't worry if they don't actually brown. Remove scallops from skillet and keep warm.

Add wine to skillet and bring to a boil. Cook until the mixture is reduced to a few syrupy spoonfuls. Whisk in the mustard and the crème fraîche or heavy cream and boil for 2 minutes. Taste sauce and correct seasoning. Arrange scallops on a serving platter or on plates and spoon sauce over them. Sprinkle with chopped tomato and serve immediately.

Crème Fraîche (for above recipe)

1 cup heavy cream (not ultra pasteurized)
1 cup dairy sour cream

Whisk heavy cream and sour cream together in bowl. Cover loosely with plastic wrap and let stand on counter overnight or until thickened. Cover and refrigerate for at least 4 hours, after which the crème fraîche will be quite thick. The tart flavor will continue to develop as the crème fraîche sits in the refrigerator. Makes 2 cups.

Alain Bernier
Westmoreland, New Hampshire

VENISON STEAK WITH BARBECUE SAUCE

1½ lbs. venison steaks
1 cup barbecue sauce
1 medium onion, sliced
4-6 slices uncooked bacon, diced
¼ cup brown sugar
¼ cup water

Place steaks in 2½-quart casserole dish; mix remaining ingredients and pour over steaks. Cover and bake at 350° for 1½ hours.

Heath Marmion
Carthage, Illinois

CHICKEN FRIED VENISON STEAK

2 lbs. venison steaks, sliced ¼-½" thick
1 can evaporated milk
  salt and pepper
  garlic powder
  onion powder
  flour
  cooking oil

Pound venison into thin strips. Place in shallow dish and cover with evaporated milk (add water as needed to cover meat); set aside for 1½ hours. Drain meat, sprinkle seasonings to taste and roll meat in flour to coat.

Coat bottom of large skillet with oil; heat oil over medium-high heat. Add meat to hot oil, and lightly brown both sides until tender. Don't overcook!

For gravy, add flour to pan drippings and brown slightly. Add milk or water and heat until thick.

Randy Bacon
Avon, Colorado

SLOW-COOKED SKILLET TENDERLOIN

venison tenderloin, cut
into 1/2-3/4"-thick slices
1 cup flour
pinch of salt
1 T. garlic pepper

1 egg, beaten
1/2 cup margarine
3 medium onions, sliced
milk and flour

Mix flour, salt and garlic pepper together in a plastic bag. Set aside. Beat the egg in a bowl. Dip pieces of tenderloin in egg. Put into plastic bag and shake to coat with flour mixture. Heat electric skillet at 400° and melt margarine.

Place tenderloin pieces in skillet and brown quickly on each side. Reduce heat to simmer and let simmer for 45 minutes. Add onions while simmering, and turn meat occasionally. Remove meat and onions; add milk and flour to leftover drippings to make desired amount of gravy. Serve with mashed potatoes and corn.

Richard Harvey
Chambersburg, PA

CHRIS' VENISON BARBECUE

2 lbs. lean venison, cut
into 1/2" cubes
8 strips bacon
1 cup red wine vinegar
1 cup packed dark brown sugar

2 large onions, diced
2 cups ketchup
1 12 oz. can beer
salt and pepper to taste

In a large pot, fry the bacon until crisp; remove, crumble and set aside. Add the cubed venison to the bacon grease in several small batches, browning well. Remove venison and set aside.

Add remaining ingredients to the drippings in the pot, stir well, and simmer for 10-15 minutes. Return venison and crumbled bacon to the mixture, cover, and simmer 30-40 minutes. I prefer this served over white rice, but it should be as good over noodles or maybe even bread or biscuits.

William C. Rogers
Summerfield, North Carolina

BARBECUE VENISON SOUTHERN STYLE

This recipe will allow you to use all those bone scraps and trimmings immediately after processing your deer, or you can freeze them for later use

	meaty bones and scraps from one deer
2½	lbs. onions, sliced ¼" thick and cut in half
	salt and pepper to taste
	minced garlic to taste
2	cans beer
½-1	gal. barbecue sauce

Place all bones and scraps in the largest pot you have and cook until the meat falls from the bones. Remove from heat and cool completely; this will allow that unwanted tallow to solidify for easy removal.

Shred meat and place it in a large enough pot to allow you to double its bulk. Add onions, garlic and salt and pepper to taste; add two cans of your favorite beer. Combine all ingredients with your favorite barbecue sauce, adding enough to allow for cooking down all day.

Simmer contents of pot over low heat for several hours, stirring occasionally. This can be frozen or canned, and is great any time of the year, served any style you wish.

Russell Hardick
Dundee, New York

GRILLED RUBBED VENISON TENDERLOIN

- 1 whole tenderloin
- 2 T. Worcestershire sauce
- 1 T. dried parsley
- 1 tsp. garlic powder
- 1 tsp. paprika
- 1/2 tsp. salt
- 1/2 tsp. fresh cracked pepper
- 1/4 tsp. cayenne pepper
  sautéed onions (optional)

Peel or cut away any fat or membrane from the tenderloin. Rub tenderloin with Worcestershire sauce. Mix together all dry ingredients and rub on tenderloin evenly. Let stand for 30-40 minutes

Grill over medium heat until medium-well done. You don't want to cook this well done, because meat will dry out. When done, slice ¾ inch thick per serving. Also good with sautéed onions served on top of each slice.

Can also be prepared in oven. Roast at 325° until done, about 22 minutes per pound for medium-well.

Janet S. Oursler
Jessup, Maryland

SPICED HICKORY RIBS

4 lbs. venison
1½ tsp. ground ginger
1½ tsp. ground coriander
½ tsp. paprika
½ tsp. salt

¼ tsp. pepper
½ cup peach preserves
½ cup beer
hickory chips

Combine ginger, coriander, paprika, salt and pepper; rub into meaty sides of ribs. Cover and chill for 2 hours. About 1 hour before cooking time, cover hickory chips in water and soak. Arrange hot coals on both sides of foil drip pan. Drain hickory chips. Sprinkle some over coals.

Lace ribs accordion style on spit rod. Secure holding forks on spit and attach spit to grill. Position drip pan under meat. Turn on rotisserie and grill ribs over medium coals for 1 hour, or until done. Sprinkle coals with hickory chips every 20 minutes. In blender, blend preserves and beer until smooth. Brush mixture onto ribs during last 10 minutes of grilling to glaze.

Joe Nuciola
Albion, New York

BREADED VENISON CHOPS

3 lbs. boneless venison chops
2-3 cups Italian bread crumbs
3 large eggs

1 cup flour
1 cup olive oil

Put crumbs in a large bowl, put eggs in another bowl, put flour in a third bowl. Heat olive oil in large frying pan. Dip chops in flour, then in egg, and then in bread crumbs.

Place chops in frying pan and cook for 15 minutes. When done, serve with ketchup or steak sauce. Serve with vegetables, for a quick meal that tastes great.

Joe Nuciola
Albion, New York

SLOW COOKER VENISON BURGUNDY

2-4 lb. venison sirloin tip or rump roast
2 pkgs. beef au jus mix
1½ cups hot water
 burgundy wine (optional)
1 cup mushrooms, sliced (optional)
1 medium onion, sliced (optional)
2 T. cornstarch

Place venison in slow cooker. Add both packages au jus mix to 1½ cups hot water and stir until completely dissolved. Pour liquid over roast. Add burgundy wine or more water to cover roast. Add mushrooms and sliced onion if desired. Cook on low for 6-8 hours, depending on size of roast. The roast can remain in slow cooker longer if covered with liquid to prevent it from drying out.

Remove roast from slow cooker and place on cutting board. Remove onion and mushrooms from liquid; reserve liquid. Pour liquid into a saucepan and allow to cool about 5 minutes. Dissolve cornstarch in ¼ cup water, and add to onion and mushroom liquid. Cook over medium heat until thickened.

Slice roast and place on serving platter with some of the sauce ladled over the venison. Pour remainder of the sauce into a gravy boat. Serve with a green vegetable and mashed potatoes or noodles.

William C. Meyer
Sandwich, Illinois

SCHNITZEL

venison round steak
1 egg, beaten
½ cup milk
2 cups crushed soda cracker crumbs
salt and pepper to taste

Beat egg and milk together; dip steaks in mixture, then coat with crumbs. Fry in melted butter golden brown. Add salt and pepper to taste. Bake at 350° for about 1 hour. Schnitzel goes well with fried potatoes or your favorite baked or mashed potatoes.

Mrs. Clayton R. Kauer
Rib Lake, Wisconsin

HERB AND ONION VENISON TENDERLOIN

2½ lbs. tenderloins, trimmed
2 tsp. oil
2 cups sliced onions
2 cloves garlic, minced
½ tsp. dried rosemary
½ tsp. dried thyme leaves
¼ tsp. salt
⅛ tsp. pepper

Spray roasting rack with cooking spray and place in roasting pan. Cut tenderloins lengthwise, almost to, but not through opposite side. Open tenderloins like a book so each lies flat and place on prepared rack.

Spray large nonstick skillet with cooking spray. Add oil and heat over medium-high heat; sauté onions and garlic in hot oil until tender. Stir in rosemary, thyme, salt and pepper. Spread onion mixture evenly over tenderloins. Bake at 375° for about 40 minutes or until meat is no longer pink.

Donald E. Hayes
Jefferson, Wisconsin

SMOKED VENISON

A covered barbecue grill or smoker grill is required to properly prepare this recipe. This was a popular recipe in our deer camp.

2 lbs. venison hindquarter
   garlic salt
   lemon pepper

1 lb. thick-sliced bacon
  kitchen string
  hickory chips, soaked

Cut the venison into serving size slices, sprinkling each piece liberally with garlic salt and lemon pepper. Fry eight pieces of bacon; rub each piece of venison with bacon drippings. Attach one piece of uncooked bacon to each piece of meat with a toothpick. Layer venison slices with one bacon slice between them to form one large roast. Secure roast with kitchen string.

Start the charcoal fire in the grill. Add hickory chips to the fire when the coals are gray. Place the meat on a rack over the charcoal and cover the grill. Smoke at 190° to 210° for 2 hours, adding charcoal as necessary. Continue cooking until meat is medium-rare.

George Hamilton
Oldsmar, Florida

WORKING MAN (OR WOMAN) STEAK

1 lb. or more venison
   steak
3/4 cup flour
   shortening
4-5 cups water
1/2 cup onion, chopped

1/4 cup green bell pepper,
   chopped
1 1/2 T. beef bouillon granules
   or 2 beef boullion cubes
   salt and pepper
   other favorite seasonings

Coat steaks with flour; fry in shortening in hot skillet. Put steak, water, onion, pepper and seasonings in a slow cooker. Turn to 300° and cook for 5-6 hours or 250° for 8 hours.

Remove 1½ cups broth. Mix with remaining flour–about ½ cup–stirring until smooth. Stir flour mixture into steak slow cooker, simmer for a few minutes , and it's ready to eat.

Charlene Losic
Reedsburg, Wisconsin

VENISON CACCIATORE

1   lb. venison steaks
    vegetable oil
2   onions, chopped
2   clove garlic, minced
1/4 tsp. pepper
1   large can stewed tomatoes
1   small can tomato paste combined
    with 1 cup of water
1/2 cup fresh chopped parsley
1   tsp. dried oregano
3   T. sugar
1/2 cup red wine (optional)
5   cups cooked rice

Fry venison steaks in oil in a large skillet or electric fry pan. When done, place on paper towels to drain. Add the chopped onion to remaining oil in skillet and cook until it is dark golden brown. Add the garlic and pepper to the pan. Cook until the mixture is well browned.

Cut the venison steaks into bite-size pieces and put them in the skillet. Add the stewed tomatoes, tomato paste mixture, parsley, oregano, sugar and wine. Bring the mixture to a boil, reduce heat and simmer for 10-15 minutes. Spoon the cooked rice onto individual plates and then ladle the venison cacciatore onto the rice.

Bruce J. Alpart
Ghent, New York

VENISON STEW AND DUMPLINGS

	venison stew meat, cubed
1/4	cup all-purpose flour
1 1/2	tsp. salt
1/2	tsp. pepper
3	T. vegetable oil or shortening
5	cups water
1	tsp. sugar
1	tsp. Worcestershire sauce
1	clove garlic, minced
1	small bay leaf
6	small potatoes, halved
6	medium carrots, halved
6	small onions
2	ribs of celery, including leaves, cut into chunks
3	cups sliced fresh mushrooms
1	cup diced zucchini
3	T. milk
1	egg
1	cup buttermilk baking mix

Combine flour, salt and pepper. Dredge meat cubes in mixture. Brown coated cubes in hot oil in a kettle. Stir in next five ingredients; cover, reduce heat and simmer for about 2 hours. Add potatoes, carrots, onions, celery, mushrooms and zucchini. Cover and cook over low heat for about 15 minutes. Combine milk, egg, and baking mix in small bowl. Stir until all ingredients are moistened. Drop dough by tablespoons on top of stew. Cook uncovered over low heat 10 minutes. Cover and cook another 10 minutes. Serve hot.

Jeff Bajczyk
Eagle, Wisconsin

JEFF'S GARDEN VARIETY VENISON SPAGHETTI

½ lb. ground venison
½ lb. Italian sausage, crumbled
2 small cans diced tomatoes
1 small can tomato paste
2 T. olive oil
2 medium onions, diced
1-2 carrots, peeled and diced fine
1-2 ribs celery, diced fine
3-4 cloves garlic, chopped or minced
1 green bell pepper, diced
½ cup or more diced fresh mushrooms
½ cup or more diced fresh zucchini squash
½ cup or more chopped fresh spinach
1 tsp. sugar
1 beef bouillon cube
½ tsp. black pepper
½ cup chopped fresh parsley or 1 tsp. dried parsley
4 T. chopped fresh basil or 2 tsp. dried basil
1 tsp. dried oregano
½ tsp. dried thyme
1 bay leaf
1 tsp. salt-free seasoning

Remove casings from sausage links, crumble into frying pan and brown with ground venison. Drain and transfer to slow cooker along with tomatoes and tomato paste.

Heat oil in large skillet or Dutch oven. Add remaining vegetables and cook until tender; transfer to slow cooker. Cook at medium heat for 2 hours or more (the longer the better), stirring occasionally. Remove bay leaf and serve over 1 pound spaghetti noodles, cooked according to package directions. Sprinkle with Parmesan cheese to taste.

Jeff Bajczyk
Eagle, Wisconsin

BARBECUED VENISON RIBS

	venison ribs	2	T. lemon juice
1	cup chili sauce	1/2	tsp. salt
1 1/2	cups water	1	tsp. cornstarch dissolved
1/2	cup Worcestershire		in water
	sauce		chili powder to taste

Combine chili sauce, water, Worcestershire sauce, lemon juice and salt in a small saucepan. Bring to a boil, then simmer 5 minutes. Slowly add cornstarch and water to thicken. Remove sauce from heat.

Wipe any dried blood from inside of rib cage. With a bone saw, cut each side of rib cage in half at right angle to ribs, then saw off the backbone. Cut these half-racks into plates of 3-4 ribs each. Discard any bloodshot or broken ribs. Allow one or two plates per person.

Place ribs on a rack with a shallow pan or foil beneath them to catch drippings. Roast at 400° for 10-20 minutes to remove excess tallow. Transfer ribs to a roasting pan and baste liberally with barbecue sauce. Reduce heat to 350° and roast ribs, basting with sauce and turning frequently, until tender. Or, better yet, grill ribs over indirect heat. Baste liberally barbecue sauce. Serve with mashed potatoes and sliced carrots.

Jeff Bajczyk
Eagle, Wisconsin

VENISON WITH RED GRAVY

1	lb. venison loin steaks or round steaks	1	small onion, diced
2	cans tomato soup	1/2	green bell pepper, diced
3	carrots, cut into bite-size pieces	2	T. barbecue sauce
		1	T. ketchup
			salt and pepper to taste

Brown the meat in butter in a skillet. Place all meat and remaining ingredients in a roaster and bake at 350° for about 1 1/2 hours. Serve over rice.

Jeff Bajczyk
Eagle, Wisconsin

JEFF'S DEEP-DISH LASAGNA

1/2	lb. ground venison	1	10-oz. package frozen
1/2	lb. bulk sausage		chopped spinach
2/3	cup chopped onion	2	cups or less water
2/3	cup chopped parsley	16	oz. Ricotta cheese or
1/2	T. minced garlic		cottage cheese
3	6-oz. cans tomato paste	1/2	cup grated fresh
1	15-oz. can tomato sauce		Parmesan
1 1/2	tsp. dried oregano	3	eggs
1 1/2	tsp. dried sweet	12	lasagna noodles,
	basil leaves		cooked according
1 1/2	tsp. Italian seasoning		to package directions
2	tsp. garlic salt	3	cups shredded
1/4	tsp. pepper		Mozzarella cheese

In kettle or soup pot, brown venison, sausage, onion, half the parsley and garlic; drain. Add tomato paste, tomato sauce, seasonings, spinach and some of the water. Mix well; cover and simmer for at least 5 minutes, stirring occasionally.

Meanwhile, in a bowl, combine the remaining parsley, Ricotta cheese, Parmesan and eggs; mix well. In a lightly greased 13x9x2 inch baking dish, spread a thin layer of the tomato sauce. Lay 4 noodles, 1/3 of the cheese mixture, 1/3 of the remaining sauce mixture and one cup of the Mozzarella cheese. Repeat layering ending with noodles, sauce, cheese and Mozzarella cheese on top.

Cover with aluminum foil and bake at 350° for 45 minutes, uncover and bake for 10 minutes more or until cheese just starts to brown. Let cool 10 minutes before serving.

Preferred alternative: Instead of 2 cups water, use 1-2 cups diced zucchini squash plus the water used to rinse out the tomato paste and tomato sauce cans.

Jeff Bajczyk
Eagle, Wisconsin

BEST-EVER SLOW-COOKER VENISON STROGANOFF

2 lbs. stewing venison cubed	3 cloves garlic, minced
2 cans beef consommé	3 juniper berries crushed
2 cups red wine	
½ cup flour mixed with seasoned salt and pepper	1 tsp. dried thyme
	1 tsp. mustard powder
5 T. shortening	
1 large yellow onion, halved and thinly sliced	1 tsp. cracked black pepper
1 lb. crimini or button mushrooms, halved or quartered	2 cups sour cream
	1 lb. uncooked extra-wide egg noodles
1 large carrot, grated	

Pour the consommé and wine into slow cooker and turn it on. Dredge the venison in the seasoned flour and coat well, shaking off excess through a colander. Heat the shortening in a large heavy frying pan until very hot but not smoking, and brown the venison deeply in batches; this step is important and should not take long if your pan is hot enough. Add the venison to the slow cooker as it is browned.

When meat is done, add the onion, and turn down the heat to medium-low; cook until onion is limp and translucent. While the onion cooks, add the mushrooms, carrot, garlic, juniper berries, thyme, mustard and black pepper to the slow cooker; then add the onions, scraping the pan for all the browned bits on the bottom. Put on the lid on the slow cooker and go hunting for more venison.

When you return 8-12 hours later, your house will smell fabulous. Stir in the sour cream and let it cook with the lid off while you prepare the noodles according to package directions. Add cooked noodles to the stroganoff; at least 30 minutes longer so the noodles can soak up the sauce. This is a killer meal served with sweet and sour beets and sourdough bread.

Andi Flanagan
Kodiak, Alaska

ITALIAN VENISON

4-5	lb. venison roast	½	tsp. ground nutmeg
2	cups water	½	tsp. black pepper
2	beef bouillon cubes	¼	tsp. dried sweet basil
1	tsp. dried oregano	⅛	tsp. dried thyme
1	tsp. fennel seed	⅛	tsp. ground allspice
½	tsp. garlic powder	1	large onion, sliced

Trim fat off meat. Place roast, water and spices in slow cooker and cook on high for 4 to 5 hours. Add the onion in the last hour of cooking. Carve roast and serve on steak buns. This is great with sliced jalapeño peppers.

John M. Drone
Mount Carmel, Illinois

SPICED VENISON POT ROAST

This recipe produces a very different taste in venison and could be used for moose, bear or anything else you can get in the pot. This combination of spices is wicked powerful, so measure carefully–especially the cardamom.

3-4	lb. bone-in venison roast, such as chuck or shoulder	½	tsp. ground cardamom
		½	tsp. ground cinnamon
		½	tsp. ground allspice
2	medium onions, sliced	½	tsp. ground nutmeg
1	tsp. salt	½	tsp. garlic powder
3	bay leaves	½	tsp. black pepper

Place roast in large pot and cover with water. Add remaining ingredients. Bring to a boil. Reduce heat, and simmer gently until done, about 3 hours, adding water as necessary to maintain level. Drain and thinly slice roast. Meat should be pink on inside from the spices, not from being rare.

Chris Burgess
Leeds, Maine

BACON WRAPPED VENISON FILLETS

Start by removing backstraps from animal. Remove all fat and sinew from backstraps (easily done with a fillet knife). Cut backstraps into pieces 4-6 inches long. Season all sides of meat chunks with your favorite seasoning.

Wrap 2-3 pieces of bacon around each piece of meat and secure with toothpicks. Cook vertically on a medium-hot grill about 10 minutes per side for medium rare. Hint: the less they cook, the more tender they will be.

This is just as good with elk, antelope, or moose. Serves 4 adults if you can keep their hands off until their plates have been filled with other food first. My kids would eat these and leave everything else if we didn't make them eat vegetables before they have seconds.

Anthony "Tony" Taylor
Willard, Missouri

VENISON WITH GRAVY

Cut venison meat into no more than ½ inch slices. Coat slices with flour and brown in small amount of oil. After meat is brown, place it in casserole dish and pour cream of mushroom soup over top. Bake at 350° for 30 minutes. Delicious with homemade biscuits.

Terry Todd
Jefferson City, MO

BACKSTRAP OR STEAK MARINADE

        venison backstrap or steaks
        lemon-lime soda
²/₃ cup soy sauce
 1   onion, sliced
 1   tsp. garlic, minced
 1   tsp. black pepper
 2   tsp. sesame seeds, toasted (optional)

Put backstrap or steak in bowl and cover with soda. Combine remaining ingredients and pour over meat; refrigerate overnight. Drain marinade and grill venison to desired doneness. You can brush venison with your favorite barbecue sauce while grilling, if you like.

Jerry and Hope Brensinger
Mt. Home, Idaho

LAZY MAN'S CASSEROLE

1¹/₂ lbs. venison, elk, moose or beef steaks, cubed
 1   can cream of mushroom soup
 1   can cream of chicken soup
 1   pkg. onion soup mix
¹/₂ cup water
 1   cup sliced mushrooms

Mix all ingredients in large casserole dish and bake at 250° for 3-4 hours, or until meat is tender. Serve over cooked noodles or mashed potatoes.

Carl Bartelt
Hillsboro, Wisconsin

CARL'S VENISON STEAKS

6 venison, elk or moose round steaks
  fat for frying
3 T. flour
1½ tsp. salt
¼ tsp. dried marjoram leaves
1 small onion, peeled and sliced
4 medium carrots, peeled and sliced
½ cup celery, chopped, with tops
1½ cups beef broth

Mix flour, salt and marjoram, and rub over meat. Brown steaks in hot fat; add vegetables and broth to pan. Cover and cook until steaks are done and vegetables are tender. Serve hot.

Carl Bartelt
Hillsboro, Wisconsin

BAKED VENISON SHOULDER

1 venison shoulder
1 bottle burgundy wine
1 tsp. dried basil
½ tsp. ginger powder
2 T. lemon juice
1 T. flour
½ stick butter, melted

Cover shoulder with burgundy wine and refrigerate for 24 hours, turning meat at least once. Mix remaining ingredients and pour over roast. Cover roast with foil and bake at 350° for 3 hours.

Kenneth W. Crummett
Sugar Grove, West Virginia

HUNGARIAN VENISON

This is a variation of a basic stroganoff, but with just enough difference to make it a little exotic. I think it probably originated as a peasant dish. Anyway, it's good.

1 lb. venison, cut into 1" cubes
2 tsp. olive oil or olive oil/butter mixture flour
1 medium onion, coarsely chopped
2 cloves garlic, crushed
¼ cup black currants or cranberries
 dry red wine
1 cup sour cream (or yogurt/cottage cheese
  mixture, if you are concerned about using that
  much sour cream)
 paprika
 black pepper
 parsley

Remove any fat and silverskin from the venison. Heat olive oil in large skillet over high heat. Dredge venison in flour, and sauté in skillet until brown. Add onion and garlic, stirring until onion becomes translucent.

Add remaining ingredients, using about half a cup of wine to start with. Stir, cover and reduce heat to simmer. Cook about 30 minutes, until done, checking a couple of times while it is cooking. This is not supposed to be soupy, so use the wine to adjust dish to the desired consistency. Garnish with parsley, add a bit more paprika for color, and serve.

You may wish to serve this with boiled potatoes or over rice. I would probably also serve a fairly robust red wine–maybe something Hungarian, in keeping with the theme.

Keith Baker
Falls Church, Virginia

CHERRIED VENISON

I know this sounds strange, but try it before you condemn it. It has the multiple virtues of seeming exotic, being easy to fix and tasting good. So, what's not to like?

- 4 venison chops, preferably boneless
- 1 tsp. olive oil
- 1 can pitted, tart cherries (or sweet cherries, if you are so inclined)
- ¼ cup slivered almonds
- 6 whole cloves
- 1 T. vinegar
  black pepper to taste

Remove any fat and silverskin from the venison. Heat olive oil in a skillet and lightly brown chops. Mix remaining ingredients and pour over the chops. (Some brands of canned cherries are fairly colorless; if you get pale cherries and want to brighten this dish up, add a bit of red food coloring.)

Cover and simmer for about 30 minutes. Place the chops on plates, and cover with the sauce. Garnish with parsley if you like. What you serve as side dishes depends on whether you have made this in the sweet or the tart version.

Keith Baker
Falls Church, Virginia

REAL TEXAS DEER CHILI

1   3-lb. venison hindquarter, cubed the size of
     sugar cubes
2   T. vegetable oil
2   large onions, chopped
6   cloves garlic, peeled and chopped
1   can beer
1   can diced tomatoes with green chilies
3   T. chili powder
1½   T. ground cumin
1   tsp. black pepper
1   tsp. meat tenderizer
½   tsp. paprika
½   tsp. celery salt
½   tsp. salt
¼   tsp. cayenne (red) pepper
¼   tsp. rubbed sage
¼   tsp. dried oregano
¼   tsp. dried thyme
¼   tsp. ground coriander

Using a large cast iron skillet, heat oil; brown venison in hot oil. Remove the browned meat and set aside. Add onions and garlic to the skillet and sauté until soft.

Return meat to the skillet and add remaining ingredients, stirring well. Cook for 15 minutes over medium heat. Reduce heat to low, cover and simmer for 45 minutes, stirring occasionally. Add more beer if chili becomes too dry.

Ronald Perry
Alvin, Texas

MARINADE FOR VENISON STEAK

This marinade will turn 2-year-old mule venison round steak into a mouth-watering delight.

4-6 venison steaks
1½ cup salad oil
¾ cup soy sauce
¼ cup Worcestershire sauce
½ cup regular or garlic wine vinegar
⅓ cup concentrated lemon juice
2 T. dry mustard
2¼ tsp. salt
1 T. dry parsley
2 large garlic cloves, minced

Be sure to trim tallow and gristle from meat before marinating. Combine all ingredients, except venison, in bowl. Add steaks; marinate overnight in refrigerator, turn occasionally.

This recipe makes a great marinade for beef flank steak or goose breast. Marinate flank steak same length of time as venison; 2 hours is adequate for thickly sliced goose breast.

Richard J. Carr
Detroit Lakes, Minnesota

Herb-Barbecued Venison Ribs

venison ribs
1   cup sugar
¼   cup white vinegar
¼   cup salt
    slice of onion
¼   tsp. chili powder
    flour
1   onion, chopped
1   small can tomato juice
½   tsp. dried oregano
½   tsp. dried basil
½   tsp. dried marjoram
1   rib celery, chopped
1   carrot, chopped

Clean fat from ribs. Combine next five ingredients; pour mixture over ribs and marinate ribs overnight in refrigerator. Pat ribs dry and coat with flour; fry in a skillet in hot oil until light brown. Remove from skillet and arrange in baking pan.

Mix remaining ingredients to make barbecue sauce. Cover ribs with sauce, bake at 350° until tender.

Arthur McClearn
Cresson, Pennsylvania

CASH'S FIVE-ALARM CHILI

1½ lbs. ground venison burger
1½ lbs. ground venison sausage
¼ cup olive oil
2 T. Worcestershire sauce
1 T. salt
1 can kidney beans
1 large can crushed tomatoes
1½ large onions, chopped
1 cup water
½ cup dry red wine
¼ cup hot pepper sauce
¼ cup crushed red pepper flakes
¼ cup chili powder
1 T. horseradish
2 tsp. ground cumin
2 tsp. parsley flakes
2 tsp. black pepper
1 tsp. garlic powder
1 tsp. liquid smoke

Brown burger and sausage in a deep pan with olive oil, Worcestershire sauce and salt. Mix remaining ingredients together in a large slow cooker. Once the meat is browned, pour contents of pan into the slow cooker. Stir well and cook on low for 4-6 hours, the longer the better.

Glenn Jourdan
Wilmington, Delaware

BUFFET MEATBALLS

1½ lbs. ground venison
2 cups sour cream, divided
2 T. ketchup
1½ tsp. salt, divided
¼ tsp. pepper
½ tsp. garlic salt
½ tsp. dried oregano
1 T. vegetable oil
1 T. water
2 tsp. dill weed
  paprika

Combine venison, ¼ cup sour cream, ketchup, 1 tsp. salt, pepper, garlic salt and oregano. Shape into 1 inch meatballs. Brown meatballs in skillet in hot oil; pour off any excess oil. Add water, cover and simmer for 15 minutes.

Remove meatballs to a chafing dish or casserole, and keep warm. Combine remaining sour cream, salt and dill in the skillet in which the meatballs were cooked. Heat through and pour over the meatballs. Sprinkle with paprika. Serve with rice or noodles.

Paul A. Garceau
Meriden, Connecticut

MIKE'S WHITE-TAIL BACKSTRAP

1 whole backstrap
  Italian salad dressing
1 small cabbage, sliced
1-2 red onions, sliced
2-4 smoked sausages
1 can spicy tomatoes
1 can cream of mushroom soup
2-3 apples, cored and sliced

Marinate backstrap overnight in Italian salad dressing. Layer 3 large sheets of aluminum foil; place half of cabbage and red onions in center of foil. Place the backstrap on the cabbage along with your favorite smoked sausages.

Mix tomatoes and soup together and pour over meat. Finish with remaining cabbage and apples over the top. Wrap completely in foil, pinching seams tightly. Grill on low heat for 2 hours. Or you can also bake packet at 350° in the oven.

Michael McCain
Cleveland, Mississippi

TERIYAKI VENISON KABOBS

6-8 oz. venison tenderloin,
sliced ¼" thick
½ cup water
2 T. soy sauce
1 T. molasses
1 tsp. dried mustard
½ tsp. ground ginger

3 cloves garlic, minced
cherry tomatoes
onion chunks
red or green bell
peppers
other vegetables of
your choice

Marinate the meat in water, soy sauce, molasses, mustard, ginger and garlic for ½ hour. Skewer meat along with vegetables as desired. Grill or broil kabobs 4-5 inches from heat source for 4-7 minutes. Brushing with marinade 3-4 times, turning the skewers each time. Warm the marinade and serve with the kabobs.

J. Nelson
River Falls, Wisconsin

PHIL'S GOULASH

2 lbs. ground venison
1 large onion, chopped
fine
1 lb. uncooked elbow
macaroni
3 qts. tomato juice

3 T. chili seasoning
blend
¼ tsp. salt
black pepper to taste
2 15 oz. cans dark red
kidney beans, drained

Brown venison in a skillet with onion; drain and set aside. In a large pot, prepare macaroni as directed on package. Drain water; add venison and remaining ingredients, except kidney beans. Simmer, uncovered for 20 minutes. Add beans to pot. Simmer for 10 minutes more.

Phil Bard
Auburn, Indiana

SCOTT'S SWEET AND SPICY JERKY

2-3 lbs. venison, sliced into ⅛ -¼" strips"
2 cups water
¾ cup brown sugar
½ cup hot soy sauce
⅓ cup vinegar
½ cup barbecue sauce
2 T. salt
1 T. hot pepper sauce
1 tsp. ground allspice
1 tsp. garlic powder
1 tsp. ginger powder
1 tsp. chili powder
½ tsp. mustard powder
pinch dried thyme
½ tsp. liquid smoke
whiskey to taste (optional)
½ cup of your favorite prepared marinade (optional)

Mix all ingredients; marinate the meat in the mixture for 12-24 hours, stirring occasionally. Drain marinade from meat out, and let strips air dry on paper towels for 1 hour. Dry the meat, hanging, in a smoker for 8-10 hours, or until desired texture, using your favorite wood chips.

Scott Barnhart
Bensalem, Pennsylvania

VENISON ROAST WITH CARROTS AND ROSEMARY SAUCE

venison roast
1 cup dry red wine
1 cup water
3 cloves garlic, crushed
6 medium carrots, cut into 1" pieces
1 medium onion, sliced
2 ribs celery, cut into 1" pieces
2 bay leaves
1 tsp. ground cumin
1/2 tsp. dried rosemary
1 tsp. fresh lemon juice
1 tsp. Worcestershire sauce
1/2 tsp. salt
1/4 tsp. ground pepper
2 T. cornstarch
1/4 cup water

Place venison in a plastic bag or glass dish; add wine, water and garlic. Marinate in the refrigerator for 4 days, turning the bag 2-4 times each day.

Drain marinade, pat roast dry and place roast in a pan. Brown roast under broiler for 4-5 minutes on each side, or until browned. Transfer the meat to a slow cooker, and add carrots, onion, celery, bay leaves, cumin and rosemary. Cover and cook for 10 hours, or cook in the oven at 250° for the same amount of time, or until tender.

Remove the meat from pan, slice and keep warm; put the liquid in a saucepan. Add lemon juice, Worcestershire, salt and pepper to liquid. If necessary, add enough water to make 1½ cups of liquid. Mix cornstarch and ¼ cup water together and add to the liquid; cook over medium heat until sauce it thickened, stirring constantly. Strain sauce and pour over sliced meat. Serve the carrots alongside. Garnish with parsley if desired.

Victor L. Mobley
Middleboro, Massachusetts

VENISON STEAK AND SCALLOP KA-BOBS

- 1 lb. venison steak, cut into 1" pieces
- 1 lb. equal size scallops
   strips of bacon
- 1/3 cup hot and spicy oil
- 1/3 cup bold steak sauce
- 1/4 cup white vinegar
- 1 T. dried thyme
- 1 T. dried basil
- 1 T. onion powder
- 1 T. blackened seasonings
- 1 T. Worcestershire sauce
- 1 tsp. sugar

Mix all ingredients except venison, scallops and bacon in a blender to make a marinade. Put in a bowl with the venison cubes for 24 hours.

Alternate the meat and scallops on skewers. Wrap skewered meat and scallops with strips of bacon, securing with toothpicks. Grill or broil skewers until the bacon is crisp, turning skewers occasionally.

John H. Dundon, Jr.
Reading, Pennsylvania

QUICK STEAKS

   venison steaks, 1/4-1/2" thick
   bacon fat
   Worcestershire sauce to taste

Heat skillet over high heat. Melt bacon fat in skillet. Sear steaks 2 minutes on one side; turn and sear another 2 minutes. Add Worcestershire sauce to skillet and cook for 1 minute. Flip steaks to first side again for 30 seconds. Serve immediately.

Allen D. Budde
Winter, Wisconsin

DEER TO DIE FOR

1 5-lb. boneless venison roast	1 large chili pepper, seeded, deveined and chopped
1 cup plain yogurt	2 T. lemon juice
1 large onion, chopped fine	1 tsp. cayenne pepper
½ cup brown sugar	1 tsp. salt
3 cloves garlic, minced	½ tsp. ground cumin
1 large jalapeño pepper, chopped	½ tsp. dried marjoram
	½ tsp. black pepper

Place all ingredients, except meat in a blender, and mix well. Spread marinade over the venison, cover with foil and refrigerate overnight, turning venison occasionally. Place the meat in a roasting pan; bake at 450° 2 hours until done.

Steven L. Hitchens
Millsboro, Delaware

VENISON CUTLETS

1 lb. venison cutlets	2 eggs, beaten
milk	1 T. parsley flakes
1 cup Italian-seasoned bread crumbs	⅓ cup oil

Place cutlets in shallow dish, and cover with milk. Marinate cutlets in the milk overnight in the refrigerator. Beat eggs and parsley together in a bowl. Set aside.

Remove cutlets from milk; coat cutlets with bread crumbs; then dip the cutlets into egg mixture. Fry cutlets in a skillet with oil until golden brown, turning once. Remove cutlets from the skillet, and place on a rack in a baking pan. Cover the pan with aluminum foil; bake at 350° for 30 minutes.

Gary A. Brennan
Stratford, Connecticut

BUDDY'S DEER CAMP CHILI

2 lbs. ground venison
1 15-oz. can pinto beans with onions
1 15-oz. can tomato sauce
1 14½-oz. can diced tomatoes
1 pkg. of chili seasoning mix

Brown the venison in a large skillet; add remaining ingredients, stirring as you add each one. Simmer for 15-20 minutes. Serve with crackers.

Buddy Burrell
Spartanburg, South Carolina

VENISON STIR FRY

1	lb. venison meat, sliced and cut into strips	1	cup red or green peppers, cut into squares
¼	cup soy sauce	2	ribs celery, thinly sliced
⅛	tsp. garlic powder	1	T. cornstarch
½	tsp. ground ginger	1	cup water
¼	cup vegetable oil	2	tomatoes, cut into wedges
1	cup green onions, thinly sliced		

Combine soy sauce, garlic and ginger powders. Add venison strips, toss to coat, and set aside while preparing vegetables.

Heat oil in large frying pan or wok over high heat. Add venison strips and toss until browned. Reduce temperature, cover and simmer over low heat for 30 minutes Turn heat up and add onions, peppers and celery. Toss until vegetables are tender-crisp, about 10 minutes mix cornstarch with water; add to pan, stirring until thickened. Add tomatoes and heat through. Good served over hot fluffy rice.

Marvin Alderman, Jr.
Renick, West Virginia

DICK'S DEER BOURGUIGNONNE

1-2	lb. venison meat, cut into 1" cubes
4	slices bacon
2	garlic cloves, minced
1	T. flour
2	medium onions, quartered
8	oz. or more mushrooms, sliced
½	cup burgundy or other red wine
1	can golden mushroom soup
1	bay leaf
2	T. chopped fresh parsley (optional)
1	tsp. dried thyme
½	tsp. hot pepper sauce
	salt
	pepper
	cooked noodles

In a large skillet, cook the bacon until crisp; remove and reserve. Brown venison and garlic in remaining bacon grease. Add flour and stir.

Crumble the bacon into skillet, and add all remaining ingredients, except noodles. Cover and simmer for 1½ hours, stirring occasionally. Remove bay leaf, and serve over noodles.

Richard Hite
Williamsburg, Ohio

RICK'S VENISON APPETIZERS

2 lb. venison tenderloin
   butter or margarine
1 box salted crackers
1 jar hot pepper rings
1 lb. extra-sharp Cheddar cheese

Cut tenderloin into ⅛-¼ inch steaks. Cook tenderloin in a frying pan with butter or margarine until well done. Place 1 piece of steak, 1 pepper and 1 piece of cheese between 2 crackers.

Eric R. Blachek
Hallstead, Pennsylvania

VENISON IN FILO

12-14 oz. venison sausage
 ⅓ cup finely chopped onion
 1 jalapeño, finely chopped
 2 large cloves garlic, chopped
 ½ tsp. ground nutmeg
 ½ tsp. ground cinnamon
 8 oz. cream cheese filo dough

Sauté sausage, onion, garlic and jalapeño in skillet. Drain; mix with remaining ingredients in bowl. Chill.

Roll the sausage mixture into a log. Layer 6 sheets of filo dough, brushing with melted butter between layers. Place sausage mixture in the center of sheets and roll up, folding in sides. Brush with melted butter.

Place on a parchment-lined cookie sheet and bake at 375° for 15 minutes, or until browned. Cool slightly before slicing.

Mrs. Butch Gosselin
Etna, Wyoming

GARLIC-STUFFED VENISON ROAST

3-4 lb. venison or other   pepper
     game roast, trimmed   1½-2 cups water
3-4 cloves garlic, peeled   2 beef bouillon cubes
     seasoned salt

Place the roast on a rack in medium-size roaster or Dutch oven. Make
3 or 4 slits about 1½ inch deep in the top of the roast, and stuff garlic
cloves into slits. Rub roast with seasoned salt and pepper; add water
and bouillon cubes to pan.

Cover and bake at 325° for 2½-3 hours, or to desired doneness. Or you
may cook in a slow cooker by bringing the broth to a boil, reducing the
heat, and simmering for 4-5 hours.

Peeled carrots and potatoes or other vegetables may be added in the
last 1½ hours of cooking time. Broth can be thickened to form a gravy.

Sonny Van
Roosevelt, Utah

GAME IN A BAG

1   3-lb. venison roast, quail, duck, pheasant or
     other wild meat
1   large oven-cooking bag
1   pkg. dry onion soup mix
1   orange, peeled and cut up
½   cup white wine
½   cup hot water with 1 chicken bouillon cube
     salt
     pepper

Prepare the cooking bag as directed on package, and place the meat
inside. Mix together remaining ingredients and pour over meat. Seal
bag and cut vents in the bag. Place in roasting pan. Roast at 250° for
4-6 hours.

William T. Demlow
Conover, Wisconsin

VENISON A LA CRESCENT PEAK

1   3-lb. venison roast, trimmed

Marinade:
3   cups dry red wine
1   cup cider vinegar
2   cups water
¼   cup pickling spice
1   large onion, quartered
2   carrots and 2 stalks celery, cut into large chunks
2   cloves garlic

For later:
2   cans of chicken broth
3   T. olive oil
½   cup flour

Heat all marinade ingredients in pot. DO NOT BOIL. Place meat and hot marinade into large pyrex bowl or stainless steel pot. Cover, let cool, then refrigerate for two or three days. If roast is not completely covered with the marinade, turn meat once a day.

Strain marinade and save. Wipe all spices off meat, place meat in strainer for ½ hour. Discard vegetables and spices. Preheat oven to 350°. Heat olive oil in a roasting pan over high heat (I prefer a covered cast iron one). Quickly brown both sides of the roast. Add 2 cups of the saved marinade plus one can of chicken broth. (If available, sprinkle meat with 1 table-spoon game seasoning, otherwise add salt and pepper to taste.) Cover roasting pan, and bake in oven for 2½ hours. Turn meat once every hour and add another ½ cup of the saved marinade.

When roast is done, place meat on ovenproof platter and keep warm in oven (cover with foil). In a glass jar, combine remaining 1 can chicken broth and the flour. Shake vigorously to avoid lumps. Bring liquid in roasting pan to a boil, scraping sides and bottom of pan. Add broth/flour mixture; stir until it bubbles, and gravy is desired consistency. Mashed potatoes or pasta.and red cabbage, or peas and carrots go well with this! Applesauce is a nice side dish, also. Now reminisce about the hunting trip–in our case, Crescent Peak, Nevada.

Wilbur Hulse
Searchlight, Nevada

KENTUCKY VENISON POT ROAST

1   2-3 lb. venison rump or shoulder roast
2   T. canola oil
²/₃ cup vegetable juice
¹/₂ cup finely chopped onion
¹/₂ cup finely chopped carrots
2   potatoes, chopped
2   tsp. beef bouillon granules
3   T. flour
¹/₂ cup sour cream
4   cups hot cooked noodles
    salt and pepper

In a Dutch oven, brown meat on all sides in hot oil. Stir in juice, onion, carrots, potatoes, and bouillon. Bring to boil, reduce heat. Cover and simmer for 1½-2 hours, or until tender.

Remove meat from pan. Add enough water to pan juices and vegetables to equal 2 cups. Return mixture to pan. Stir flour into sour cream. Add to pan juices. Cook and stir until thick. Season to taste with salt and pepper. Slice meat thinly and spoon sauce over it. Serve with noodles.

Robert Fout
Berea, Kentucky

BIG GAME

CHICKEN FRIED ANTELOPE STEAK

4 antelope backstrap steaks, about 1½" thick
    seasoned meat tenderizer
1 egg
½ cup milk
    seasoned flour
    cooking oil

Butterfly-cut each steak to give you a larger, ¾ inch-thick steak. Sprinkle well with seasoned meat tenderizer. Using a tenderizing mallet, pound steaks until well tenderized and thin.

Mix egg and milk together to make a thin wash. Dredge steaks in seasoned flour first, then dip in egg wash, then back into flour. Fry in hot oil quickly until steaks are golden, turning often.

Curt Farmer
Pampa, Texas

Curt Farmer

Mark E. Wilcox

NO-PEEK BEAR CASSEROLE

2   lbs. bear meat, cut into 1" cubes
1   pkg. dry onion soup mix
1   can condensed cream of mushroom soup
1   small can mushrooms
½   cup red wine
    hot cooked noodles or rice

Combine meat, soup mix, soup, mushrooms and wine in slow cooker.
Cook on low for 8-12 hours. Serve over noodles or rice.

Mark E. Wilcox
Kingston, Illinois

POTTED ELK

2 lbs. elk steaks
3 T. flour
1 tsp. salt
1/4 tsp. pepper
1/4 tsp. dried thyme
3 large onions, sliced
3 T. shortening
1 qt. boiling water
3 T. vinegar
1 T. ketchup

Mix flour, salt, pepper and thyme in small mixing bowl. Cut meat into serving size pieces. Brown sliced onions in shortening. Add meat, and brown. Sprinkle flour mixture over meat and onions in skillet and mix well. Add boiling water, vinegar and ketchup. Simmer for 2-3 hours., until meat is very tender.

Patrick Holena
Albuquerque, New Mexico

ELK STEW

2 lbs. elk meat, cubed
1 onion, chopped
2 T. oil
1 cup burgundy wine
1 can cream of mushroom soup
8 oz. fresh mushrooms, sliced
   green bell pepper, diced
   salt and pepper

In a skillet, brown meat and onion in oil. Drain off any fat. Add the wine, soup and mushrooms. Cover and simmer for 45 minutes. Add green pepper, and cook 15 minutes longer, uncovered. Add salt and pepper to taste. Serve over wild rice.

Thomas D. Clark
Chestertown, Maryland

MOOSE AND BEAN ENCHILADAS

1½ lbs. ground moose
1 large onion, chopped
1 can refried beans
¾ tsp. salt
⅛ tsp. garlic salt
⅓ cup taco sauce
2 cans enchilada sauce
12 corn tortillas
2 cups shredded Cheddar or Monterey Jack cheese

Brown moose and onion in large skillet. Drain. Stir in beans, salt, garlic salt and taco sauce; heat through. Set aside. Pour 1 can enchilada sauce in bottom of 13x9 inch baking dish.

Soften tortillas as directed on package. Place about ⅓ cup meat mixture on each tortilla and roll to enclose filling. Place seam-side-down in prepared baking dish. Pour second can enchilada sauce evenly over tortillas; cover enchiladas with cheese. Bake, uncovered, at 350° for 15 minutes, or until bubbly and hot.

Denny Ockinga
Bellingham, Washington

LATVIAN ANTELOPE

antelope fillets, 1½" thick
garlic salt or minced garlic
Worcestershire sauce
burgundy wine

Place antelope fillets in shallow dish; cover with burgundy wine. Refrigerate for 4-6 hours.

Drain wine off fillets. Sprinkle with garlic and Worcestershire sauce. Refrigerate for ½-1 hour. Repeat process for the other side. Cook on hot grill, turning only once, until fillets are medium rare; do not overcook.

T. Sulmeisters
Torrington, Wyoming

QUICK QUICHE

½ lb ground elk, venison, moose, etc. - cooked
    and drained
½ cup low-fat mayonnaise
½ cup skim milk
2 eggs, beaten slightly
1 T. cornstarch
1½ cups shredded Swiss or Cheddar cheese
½ cup sliced green onions
1 can refrigerated crescent rolls

Mix all ingredients together until well blended. Stir in cheese and green onions. Line 9 inch pie plate with crescent roll dough.

Pour meat mixture into pie plate. Bake at 350°, until firm in center. You can also add spinach, if desired. I use a springform pan lined with foil

Laurie Lunenschloss
Madison, WI

Laurie Lunenschloss

SOUTH DAKOTA ANTELOPE STEW

1½   lbs. less tender cuts of antelope,
        cut into 1" cubes
3   T. all-purpose flour
1   tsp. salt
2   T. cooking oil
½   cup chopped onion
1   clove garlic, minced
½   tsp. dried thyme
3   cups vegetable juice cocktail
1   cup water
1   beef bouillon cube
      few dashes hot pepper sauce
1½   cups diced potatoes
1½   cups sliced celery
1½   cups sliced carrot

In a plastic bag, combine flour and salt. Put meat in bag, shaking to coat. In a large saucepan, brown meat, half at a time, in hot oil.

Return all meat to saucepan; add onion, garlic and thyme. Stir in vegetable juice, water, bouillon cube, and hot pepper sauce. Bring to a boil. Reduce heat, cover and simmer 1¼ hours or until meat is nearly tender. Stir in potatoes, celery and carrot. Cover and simmer 30 minutes more.

Les Kopel
Whitewood, South Dakota

LARRY'S ELK CHILI

1	lb. elk meat, cut into chunks	4	medium tomatoes, chopped
1	large onion, finely diced	1½	cups red wine
3	ribs celery, finely diced	1½	T. chili powder
2	green bell peppers, finely diced	1	T. fresh chopped thyme
2	garlic cloves, finely diced	3	T. jalapeño sauce
4	tsp. canola oil		garlic powder
1	can red kidney beans, rinsed		hot pepper sauce

In large pot sauté diced celery, garlic, peppers and onion 2-3 minutes in oil over medium heat. Add meat; sauté until browned. Add remaining ingredients to pot; cover and simmer for 45 minutes stirring occasionally. Adjust seasoning with garlic powder and hot pepper sauce.

Larry Hulme
Union Gap, Washington

ANTELOPE TENDERLOIN

1 whole antelope tenderloin
1 cup red wine
1 cup teriyaki sauce
  juice of one lemon
1 tsp. grated fresh ginger
1 tsp. minced fresh garlic

Rinse tenderloin several times in very cold water. Mix remaining ingredients to make marinade. Place the tenderloin in the marinade for several hours or overnight, refrigerated.

Grill over high heat to medium-rare. To serve, slice tenderloin across the grain into ¹/₂ inch-thick medallions. Do not slice until ready to serve.

Curt Farmer
Pampa, Texas

BEAR STEW

1½-2 lbs. bear stew meat, or any big-game stew meat
¼ cup flour
1 tsp. dried marjoram leaves
1 tsp. salt
⅛ tsp. pepper
2 T. vegetable oil
1 small can whole tomatoes, undrained
1 cup water
1 medium onion, cut in half lengthwise, thinly sliced
½ cup chopped celery
¼ cup white wine or water
1 T. vinegar
2 cloves garlic, minced
1 bay leaf
2 medium baking potatoes, cut into 1" cubes

Remove all fat and silverskin from meat. Cut into 1 inch pieces. In large plastic food-storage bag, combine flour, marjoram, salt and pepper; shake to mix. Add meat; shake to coat. In heavy medium saucepan, heat oil over medium-high heat until hot. Add floured meat and brown, stirring occasionally.

Add remaining ingredients, except potatoes; mix well. Heat to boiling; reduce heat and cover. Simmer for 1 hour, stirring occasionally. Add potatoes to saucepan. Heat to boiling; reduce heat and cover. Simmer for about 1 hour, until meat and potatoes are tender, stirring occasionally. Discard bay leaf before serving.

Dale L. Hansen
Harlan, IA

Larry Jordan

PINEAPPLE SHEEP CHOPS

1	can crushed pineapple
1/2	cup butter, chopped
3	cups water
4	cloves garlic
1	T. sugar
1/2	tsp. pepper
1	tsp. salt
2-3	lbs. sheep chops

Arrange chops in baking dish. Top with remaining ingredients. Bake at 350° for 4 hours, adding water if necessary to keep moist.

Larry Jordan
Warren, OH

DOM AND RON'S EXCELLENT 3-BEAN MOOSE CHILI

3   lbs. coarsely ground moose (use $^3/_8$-$^3/_4$" grinding plate)

2   T. olive oil

2   large yellow onions, finely chopped

1   large green bell pepper, chopped

1   large red bell pepper, chopped

6-8   large, roasted and peeled green chilies, chopped (may substitute 2-3 cans chopped green chilies)

3   garlic cloves, crushed

3   jalapeño peppers, chopped (may substitute $^1/_2$ of 1 can chopped jalapeños)

1   large can crushed tomatoes

$^1/_4$ cup chili powder

2   T. ground cumin

2   tsp. salt

2   cans red kidney beans, drained

1   can pinto beans, drained

1   can black beans, drained

In a large cast iron Dutch oven or other large pot, sauté onions in olive oil until translucent. Add bell peppers and sauté until soft. Add ground moose and cook over low heat until meat is browned. Add remaining ingredients and heat until boiling. Reduce heat to low and simmer for 1½ hours, stirring occasionally. Garnish with grated Monterey Jack cheese and serve with cornbread.

Ronald Le Beaumont, M.D.
Cheyenne, Wyoming

CHEESY ELK BURGER BROCCOLI CASSEROLE

1½-2 lbs. ground elk venison
1 pkg. frozen Tater Tots®
1 onion, chopped
salt and pepper
2 cups fresh broccoli florets
½-1 cup milk
1 can cream of mushroom soup
1½ cups shredded Cheddar cheese

Arrange a single layer of Tater Tots in 9x13 inch baking pan, and brown in 350° oven. Brown elk and onion in skillet and drain. Season to taste with salt and pepper. Spoon meat mixture evenly over Tater Tots.

Arrange an even layer of broccoli over meat. Mix ½ cup or more milk with cream of mushroom soup. Pour evenly over broccoli. Top with shredded cheese; bake at 350° for 45 minutes or until bubbly.

Mike Ingram
Butte, MT

FALL-APART MOOSE

4 lb. moose rump roast
2 medium onions, diced
1 lb. carrots, chopped
2 cloves garlic
2 cups water

1 pkg. onion soup mix
salt and pepper
2 beef bouillon cubes
2 T. cornstarch

Place roast, onions and carrots in large slow cooker, and turn to high. Slice garlic and add to roast with water, soup mix, and salt and pepper to taste.

Cover and cook 4 hours. Drain juice into saucepan; add bouillon and bring to a boil. Add cornstarch and stir until thick and translucent. Pour sauce back into slow cooker and cook for 1 hour. Slice meat and serve.

Andrea Dearborn
Tok, Alaska

ELK PEPPER STEAKS

In all my game cookbooks (and I have plenty), I have never seen a recipe like this one. Please try it out — not only is it delicious, but it's quite an attractive dish. I'm sure you'll like it! This dish is wonderful at home, but tastes even better when you're camping out.

4 elk sirloin steaks
4 T. butter
4 T. bacon grease, divided
1 large yellow onion
1 large green bell pepper
1 large yellow bell pepper
1 large red bell pepper
4 cloves garlic, minced
6-8 fresh mushrooms, sliced
    salt
    pepper
    flour

In large skillet, heat butter and 2 tablespoons bacon grease. Slice onion and peppers into ¼ inch strips. Sauté onion in skillet until tender-crisp. Add peppers, garlic and mushrooms. Sauté mixture until peppers are tender-crisp. Reduce heat to low.

In another skillet, heat remaining 2 tablespoons bacon grease. Dredge steaks in mixture of flour, salt and pepper. Fry steaks to medium doneness. Serve each steak with a generous portion of vegetables on top. Excellent with a side dish of hot buttered parsley noodles and a glass of good Zinfandel.

Sherry Curtis
Veneta, Oregon

JÄGERTOPF (HUNTER'S STEW)

2 lbs. elk or venison meat, cubed
2 tsp. vegetable oil
1 large onion, coarsely chopped
3 medium potatoes, coarsely chopped
3 carrots, coarsely chopped
2 ribs celery, coarsely chopped
1 tsp. salt
1/8 tsp. black pepper
1 bay leaf
1 cup red wine
1 1/2 cups water, divided
3 tsp. cornstarch
2 tsp. horseradish

Heat oil in skillet and brown meat on all sides. Place meat and all drippings in slow cooker; add vegetables, salt, pepper, bay leaf, wine and 1 cup water. Cover and cook at medium to medium-high for 1 hour, stirring occasionally to prevent scorching.

Turn heat down to simmer and continue cooking 3-4 hours. Discard bay leaf and place meat and vegetables in serving bowl, leaving broth in slow cooker. Dissolve cornstarch in remaining ½ cup water, add horseradish, and then stir into broth. Cook, stirring continuously, until broth thickens. Pour broth over meat and vegetables or over boiled noodles as a side dish.

James Emerson
Clifton, Colorado

Steve Lake

EASIEST CAMP STEW EVER

1   lb. stew meat (moose, venison, antelope, or beef),
    cubed
2   tsp. Worcestershire sauce
    seasoned salt and pepper
1   large onion, cut into 1" chunks
1   large bag of frozen vegetables for stew
1   can of golden mushroom soup
2   cans of beefy mushroom soup
$1/4$ cup red wine (optional)

Season meat with Worcestershire sauce, seasoned salt and pepper. Cook meat and onion in a large pan until meat is tender (add a little water from time to time to prevent meat from drying). When meat is tender, add frozen vegetables, cans of soup, and ½ the water called for on soup cans. Simmer until vegetables are tender.

Steve Lake
Winfield, Missouri

ORIENTAL MOOSE

2-3 lbs. moose meat, cubed
1 cup flour
2 eggs, beaten
1/2 tsp. salt
1 cup butter or margarine

Sauce:
1 cup sugar
1/2 cup white vinegar
5 T. soy sauce
2 T. water
1 1/2 tsp. salt

Place moose in large mixing bowl. Add flour, eggs and salt; mix until all pieces of meat are coated with eggs and flour.

Melt butter in large Dutch oven and brown meat until crispy. Combine all sauce ingredients and pour over meat. Bake at 350° for 1 1/2-2 hours. Stir meat while baking to baste.

Steve Lake
Winfield, Missouri

BIG SPRINGS ELK DINNER (SWISS STEAK)

1½   lb. elk round steak
½   cup flour
½   tsp. salt
½   tsp. pepper
¼   cup bacon drippings
1   large onion, thinly sliced
     chopped fresh garlic or garlic powder
1   green bell pepper, slivered
½   cup uncooked white rice
1   can whole tomatoes, or 1 can spicy
     stewed tomatoes, well-drained
2   cups beef consommé or beef broth
2   T. flour
½   cup red table wine
     pinch each of dried thyme and marjoram

Trim excess fat from meat. Mix flour, salt and pepper. Coat both sides of meat with mixture. Cut meat into 4 pieces. Heat bacon drippings in a large, heavy skillet. Add meat, onion, garlic and green pepper. Cook until meat is nicely browned, turning to brown both sides. Transfer meat and vegetables to a baking dish. Sprinkle rice over meat and arrange tomatoes over the top.

Add 2 tablespoons flour to drippings in skillet and blend well. Add consommé and wine. If you used spiced stewed tomatoes, add liquid to consommé. Cook, stirring constantly, until mixture boils and thickens. Season to taste with salt, pepper, thyme and marjoram. Pour over contents of baking dish. Cover and bake at 350° for about 2 hours, or until meat is very tender.

Jesse Taylor
Happy Jack, Arizona

NORWEGIAN-STYLE DALL SHEEP STEW

When I was just 17 years old, many moons ago, my father, his good buddies and I went to Alaska to hunt for the ever-elusive dall sheep. On the first day of the hunt, Papa took down a beautiful sheep. He cut off the rump of the sheep and had me make a rump stew. I was glad to do this except for one little bitty thing; I had packed our camper with all of the necessary fixings for a week's worth of hearty camp dishes. The awful part was that I had forgotten my camp cookbook! I was too embarrassed to tell Papa, so, I invented this recipe. After I served the men their stew, everyone raved about how good it was — to my relief! Since then, this recipe has been a family favorite. One must admit that we good Norwegians are very inventive! Happy eating!

1	4-lb. dall sheep rump, trimmed and cubed
	safflower oil
1½	lbs. potatoes, peeled and chopped
1	yellow onion, chopped
1	tsp. salt
1	bay leaf (to see who does the dishes)
	dash garlic powder
1	turnip, peeled and chopped
4	large carrots, chopped
1	tsp. hot seasoned salt
	dash ground black pepper

In a large, hot skillet heat safflower oil; sear the cubed meat in hot oil. Pour off the cooking oil and drippings, set meat aside.

In a five-quart pot of hot water, combine the meat, vegetables and the seasonings; make sure the water covers all the ingredients. Cover the pot; cook for at least 1½ hours on medium heat or on a coal fire.

This dish is best served with red wine and plenty of sourdough bread. As Papa would have said, "Girl, you've done yourself mighty proud! This is a mighty good meal!"

Kaylan T. Ardora
Tacoma, Washington

Laurie Lunenschloss

OPEN-FACED BURGERS (VENISON, MOOSE, ELK, ETC.)

1 lb. ground big game meat
2 T. stick margarine, softened
1 T. Worcestershire sauce
1 tsp. salt
pepper

Mix all ingredients and spread evenly on half of 4-6 buns. Broil until meat is done. For appetizers, use small buns or cut large buns in fourths. P.S. Avocado on top is great.

Laurie Lunenschloss
Madison, Wisconsin

TEXAS SLAM BARBECUE

In Texas, hunters can harvest the Texas Grand Slam of exotic sheep. The slam is comprised of the Corsican Ram, the Texas Dall Ram and the Hawaiian Black Ram.

3-5   lb. ram roast
½   cup chopped onion
½   cup of your favorite barbecue sauce
½   cup medium salsa

Bake roast, uncovered at 350° for 2 hours. Allow to cool slightly before slicing. Line a shallow roasting pan with the sliced ram roast. Combine remaining ingredients and pour over the roast. Bake at 250° for 1 hour.

Serve with hash browns or wild rice.

Norman Ramey
Killeen, Texas

BLEU CHEESE MOOSEBURGERS

1   lb. ground moose
1   small onion, minced
½   cup soft bread crumbs
¼   cup evaporated milk
3   T. ketchup (or cranberry ketchup)
2   tsp. prepared horseradish
2   tsp. prepared mustard
1½ tsp. Worcestershire sauce
1   tsp. seasoned salt
4   oz. bleu cheese, crumbled
3   oz. cream cheese, softened
    flour for dusting

Mix all ingredients except cheeses and flour in a large bowl; divide into 8 equal portions. Mix cheeses together. Press meat portions into large, thin patties and spoon cheese equally onto the middle of 4; cover with remaining 4 patties and seal edges well.

Dust burgers lightly with flour. Broil 3 inches from heat for about 6 minutes on each side. Serve with dill pickles, sourdough bread and lots of cranberry ketchup.

Andi Flanagan
Kodiak, Alaska

CHUCK'S ZESTY BEAR TENDERS

1 2-lb. bear roast, cut into strips
2 pkgs. Italian dressing mix
2 jars pepperoncini peppers
2 cloves garlic, minced

Mix Italian dressing according to package directions. Place all ingredients in slow cooker and stir. Cook on low for 5 hours.

Chuck Webb
Columbia City, IN

Chuck Webb

AFOGNAK ELK STEAKS WITH MAPLE

4 elk steaks or chops, 1/2" thick
2 eggs, beaten
2 T. maple syrup
1 T. water
1 cup dry bread crumbs
1 tsp. onion salt
1/2 tsp. garlic powder
1/2 * tsp. cracked black pepper
1 T. lard or shortening
2 T. butter

Beat eggs with maple syrup and water. Mix crumbs with spices. Dip meat into eggs, then crumbs, then eggs again, then crumbs. Refrigerate for 30 minutes to set coating.

In a Dutch oven with a tight fitting lid, heat lard and butter until very hot, but not smoking; brown steaks well in pot. Cover and bake at 300° for 2½-3 hours. Serve with garlic mashed potatoes and petit pois peas with a little mint.

Andi Flanagan
Kodiak, Alaska

BLEU BOU

2 lbs. tender caribou, cut into 1" cubes
2 T. cooking oil
4 T. butter
¼ cup flour
1 tsp. seasoned salt
1½ cups milk
4 oz. bleu cheese, crumbled
4 T. diced red bell pepper
4 T. diced green bell pepper
8 oz. egg noodles, cooked and drained

In a heavy frying pan over medium heat, heat oil and brown meat deeply; drain and set aside. In a saucepan over medium heat, melt butter; add flour, whisking constantly. Cook for 3 minutes.

Remove from heat, and whisk in milk. Return to heat and cook, stirring constantly, until thickened.

Add cheese and stir until melted. Blend in peppers. Add meat and cheese mixture to noodles; pour mixture into a greased casserole. Bake at 350° for 40 minutes.

Andi Flanagan
Kodiak, Alaska

PIZZA-BOO

1 lb. ground caribou or moose
1/2 cup nonfat dry milk
1/2 cup dry bread crumbs
2 cloves garlic, minced
1 small onion, minced
1 cup venison or beef broth
1 cup favorite pizza sauce
1 cup Cheddar cheese, grated
    toppings = black olives, tomato, green pepper,
    mushrooms, pepperoni, etc., cut as desired
1 cup mozzarella cheese, shredded

To make meat crust, combine first six ingredients, and spread to an even thickness in a 10 inch pie pan. Combine the pizza sauce with the Cheddar cheese and spread over meat crust. Top with your favorite toppings and sprinkle mozzarella over top. Bake at 350° for 30-40 minutes or until meat crust is done. Cool 5-10 minutes before cutting.

Andi Flanagan
Kodiak, Alaska

MOOSE KAPOOSTA (RUSSIAN CABBAGE PIE)

2 cups chopped or ground cooked moose meat,
   cooked and chopped or ground
1/2 cup butter or margarine
4 cups shredded cabbage
1 medium carrot, grated
1 large onion, chopped
1 clove garlic
   salt and pepper to taste
1/2 cup minced parsley
3/4 cup water or beef broth
   pastry for 2-crust, 10" pie
   sour cream to garnish

Melt butter in a large, heavy skillet, sauté cabbage, carrot, onion, garlic, salt and pepper for 20 minutes, or until vegetables are soft and beginning to brown. Add meat and water or broth; cover and cook for 10 minutes. Line pie pan with pastry; spoon meat mixture into crust. Cover with the top crust, sealing well, and cut steam vents in top. Bake at 450° for 25 minutes or until lightly brown. Serve with sour cream.

This meal just has to include pickled beets and black rye bread for a true Russian taste experience.

Andi Flanagan
Kodiak, Alaska

ALASKA CARIBOU ROAST

2 lbs. thick caribou
    steaks
2 cloves garlic, minced
    flour
3 T. oil
    pepper
1 medium onion,
    chopped
1 cup tomato sauce
1 cup sliced black
    olives
$1/3$ cup olive oil
1 tsp. chili powder
$1/4$ tsp. dried oregano

Sprinkle one side of meat with pepper and garlic; coat with flour. Pound meat with mallet. Turn steaks and repeat.

Heat oil in skillet, and brown the *Bev Grafel*
meat, then place in casserole
dish. Brown onions in oil; add remaining ingredients to the skillet, mixing well. Pour mixture over the meat. Cover and bake at 325° for 2 hours.

Bev Grafel
Eagle River, Alaska

LORI'S ANTELOPE STEW

1 lb. antelope stewing
   meat, trimmed of
   all fat and cubed
1 can chicken broth
1 can beef broth
1 cup carrots, thickly
   sliced
1 cup celery, diced
½ green bell pepper,
   diced
1½ yellow onions, sliced
6-8 cloves garlic, peeled
   and sliced
½ tsp. Hot Shot pepper
   blend
1 tsp. summer savory
2 T. dried minced garlic
2 bay leaves
2 T. Worcestershire sauce
   dash liquid smoke

Lori Sala

   flour
   Cajun seasoning blend
2-4 cups of water
6 large mushrooms, sliced
   salt and pepper

In large cooking pot, combine chicken and beef broths; add carrots,
celery, bell pepper, half the onions and fresh garlic. Simmer for
15 minutes. Add the pepper blend, summer savory, dried garlic,
bay leaves, Worcestershire and liquid smoke. Continue simmering.

While vegetables are cooking, season flour with Cajun seasoning. Coat
antelope cakes with flour, and brown with remaining onions in small
amount of cooking oil. When the meat is nicely browned, add it to
broth and vegetables. Cook for 1 hour over medium heat, stirring
occasionally and adding water a little at a time if stew gets too thick.

Add sliced mushrooms and salt and pepper to taste during the last
20 minutes. For a variation, try adding new potatoes or rice. to stew.
Serve with hot buttered rolls and salad.

Lori Sala
Oakdale, California

Arizona Swiss Elk

1   elk round steak
    vegetable oil
1   can whole tomatoes
1   small can tomato
    sauce
½   cup chopped onion
⅓   cup chopped celery
    garlic powder
    salt and pepper

Trim fat from round steak and cut
into serving size pieces. Brown
steak in oil in large skillet; drain oil.
Chop tomatoes and add to skillet
along with juice. Add tomato
sauce, onion, celery, dash of garlic
powder, and salt and pepper to
taste. Cover and simmer over low
heat until steak is tender. Serve with
mashed potatoes and vegetable of choice. Recipe is easily doubled.

Randy H. Sifford

Randy H. Sifford
Cave Creek, Arizona

Elk and Bacon Roll-ups

elk round steak
bacon strips
garlic powder

Trim all fat from steak and pound to ¼ inch thickness with meat mallet.
Slice steak into strips about the size of a strip of bacon and sprinkle
lightly with garlic powder. Place each piece of steak on a strip of bacon
and roll up with the bacon on the outside of the roll. Secure each roll
with two toothpicks. Grill over coals in covered grill until steak is
medium rare.

Randy H. Sifford
Cave Creek, Arizona

SMOKEY BILL CARNEY'S HURT-YOURSELF ELK ROAST

This meal for a large group bastes itself, leaving the cook time for other things. Smokey Bill says this will make 8 people hurt themselves from overeating.

1	8-lb. elk roast
8	cloves garlic, peeled
1	rib celery, cut into 8 pieces
	bacon
	garlic salt
	black pepper
	parsley flakes
	paprika
	Worcestershire sauce
	bacon grease for browning roast
½	cup dry red wine
¼	cup bacon grease
1	onion, sliced
	potatoes for 8
	juice of ½ lemon

Remove all silver-skin and any fat from roast. Pierce roast 8 times with a fillet knife. In each hole, put a peeled garlic clove, a piece of celery and a bit of bacon. Rub garlic salt, pepper, parsley flakes, paprika and Worcestershire on all sides.

Lightly brown the roast in bacon grease in a large skillet to seal in juices. Place the roast in a shallow foil pan. Pour ½ cup wine along with ¼ cup bacon grease over the meat. Sprinkle with a little more garlic salt and pepper. Wrap with 3 slices of bacon and 3 slices of onion, and secure with toothpicks. Place roast in a smoker. Using a few handfuls of mesquite chips, smoke roast for about 4 hours., adding potatoes during last hour. Squeeze juice of a half lemon over roast before serving and spoon juices over every serving.

Daniel J. Richeson
Spokane, Washington

BAKED BEAR BURGERS

1½ lbs. ground bear meat
1   cup soft bread crumbs
½   cup tomato juice
1   egg, beaten
2   tsp. salt
1   tsp. chopped fresh parsley
½   tsp. grated onion
¼   tsp. pepper
4   strips bacon, halved

Combine all ingredients, except bacon and mix well. Form mixture into 4 burgers. Place into greased pan and lay bacon strips on top of burgers. Bake at 350° for 45 minutes.

Arthur McClearn
Cresson, Pennsylvania

WILD HOG CHILI

8   lbs. bulk wild hog sausage
4   T. chili powder
2   tsp. cayenne pepper
1   T. ground cumin
1   T. paprika
2   tsp. garlic
2   tsp. salt
3   small cans tomato sauce
1   tsp. dried oregano

Brown meat, and drain all but 2 tablespoons grease. Add 8 cups water and remaining ingredients, simmer over medium-high until water is nearly gone then add 2 more cups of water, stirring constantly. When remaining water is nearly gone the chili is done.

Rick Maxey
Wichita Falls, Texas

CARIBOU MEATBALLS IN MUSHROOM AND CHEESE SAUCE

1½ lbs. ground caribou
    or venison
½ cup chopped onion
½ cup chopped green
    bell pepper
3 T. butter or
    margarine, divided
1 egg
¾ tsp. salt
¼ tsp. black pepper
½ tsp. garlic powder
3 T. olive oil
3 cups sliced fresh
    mushrooms
2 T. flour
2 cups water
1 8-oz. pkg. processed
    cheese
2 T. cooking sherry

Greg E. Lattery

Sauté the onion and green pepper for 5 minutes. in 2 tablespoons butter.

Mix in large bowl, combine cooked vegetables, meat, egg, salt, pepper and garlic powder. Shape mixture into 1 inch meatballs; brown in olive oil.

To make the sauce, sauté mushrooms for 5 minutes in 1 tablespoon butter and mix with remaining ingredients. Cook until thickened and hot; add to meatballs.

Meatballs can be used as an appetizer or can be served with sauce over noodles or rice. The sauce can be used as a chip dip too.

Greg E. Lattery
St. Paul, Minnesota

SMALL GAME

ROAST RABBIT

1	rabbit, dressed	1	onion, chopped
	salt and pepper	1	carrot, chopped
½	cup ground pork	1	sprig parsley, chopped
½	cup ground beef	1	sprig thyme, crushed
1	cup bread crumbs	1	bay leaf, crushed
1	egg, beaten	½	cup milk
	flour	½	cup melted margarine

Wash rabbit and soak in lightly salted water for 1 hour or longer. Dry rabbit and rub well with salt and pepper. In a bowl combine pork, beef, bread crumbs, egg, salt and pepper. Stuff cavity of rabbit with mixture.

Dust rabbit lightly with flour, and place in roasting pan on a bed of onion, carrots, parsley, thyme and bay leaf. Moisten with hot water. Cover and roast at 300° for 2 hours basting frequently, first with milk until half done and then with melted margarine. Pour gravy over rabbit and serve.

Denny Brashears
Branch, Arkansas

HOT DAMN! RABBIT

	hindquarters and backs	½	T. hot pepper sauce
	from two large rabbits	4	fresh mushrooms, sliced
½	cup butter	4	T. dry sherry
1	T. minced garlic	4	T. paprika

Boil hindquarters and backs of rabbits for 20 minutes. Carefully remove meat from bones and cut into small chunks. Melt butter in small saucepan and add garlic and hot pepper sauce.

Spread mushrooms in bottom of medium baking dish and cover with rabbit chunks. Pour butter mixture over rabbit. Do the same with sherry. Sprinkle paprika over top. Bake in 400° oven for 15 minutes. Serve over rice or noodles.

S. Wesley Waldron
Trout Run, Pennsylvania

SWEET AND SOUR COON

1	medium to large raccoon, dressed and cut into serving-size pieces
1³/₄	cups vinegar
1	large onion, chopped
1	tsp. dry mustard
1	tsp. ground allspice
1	tsp. salt
¹/₂	tsp. pepper
4	beef bouillon cubes
4	cups water
³/₄	cup ketchup
1	T. gingerroot, peeled and very thinly sliced
³/₄	cup brown sugar

Place racoon in large pot. Add 1 cup vinegar plus enough water, to cover racoon. Bring to a boil, and boil for 3-5 minutes. After parboiling coon, remove any remaining fat, even between muscle groups; fat should look white to translucent.

Place meat pieces in a roasting pan. Add onion; combine mustard, allspice, salt and pepper, and rub into coon. In a separate pan, heat and dissolve bouillon cubes in water; add ¾ cup vinegar, ketchup, ginger, and brown sugar. Pour mixture over raccoon pieces. Roast, covered, in a 350° oven until tender, about 3 hours, basting with juices 2-3 times.

Brian R. Gage
Sioux Falls, South Dakota

BAKED SQUIRREL

4 fox or gray squirrels, dressed	1 T. dried rosemary leaves
2 cups flour	2 cups chicken gravy
½ cup Creole seasoning	1 can cream of chicken soup
2 T. seasoned salt	
1 T. seasoned pepper	½ soup can of water
½ cup vegetable oil	1 small onion, chopped
1 T. garlic powder	2 ribs celery, chopped
1 T. dried basil leaves	

Mix flour, Creole seasoning, salt and pepper in plastic bag. Cut squirrels in half; place in bag and shake until well coated. Brown squirrel in hot oil.

Mix remaining ingredients together. Place browned squirrel in roaster and pour soup mixture over squirrel. Cover and bake at 225° for 5 hours.

Tom O'Connor
Granite Falls, Minnesota

SQUIRREL WITH GARLIC

1 squirrel, dressed
2 T. butter
2 garlic cloves, chopped
½ tsp. dried thyme
½ tsp. dried rosemary
⅛ tsp. black pepper
salt to taste

Remove fat from squirrel and cut meat into pieces. In frying pan, melt butter over medium heat. Stir in garlic, thyme, rosemary, pepper and salt. When garlic is soft, add squirrel and brown for 5 minutes on one side. Turn squirrel over, cover pan and cook over low heat for 1 hour. Remove squirrel from pan and keep warm. On high heat, stir juice in pan until it thickens. Spoon sauce over squirrel.

Robert L. Wheaton
Rochester, New York

LOUISIANA FRIED RABBIT STEAKS

2 rabbits, dressed
    salt
    black pepper
    cayenne pepper
    flour
    milk
    vegetable shortening

Cut meat off the bones of rabbits and season with salt and pepper. Pound each piece thin with a meat mallet to tenderize. Season the flour to taste with salt, black pepper and cayenne pepper. Dip rabbit pieces in flour, then milk, then flour again to coat well. Deep fry in hot shortening. These little steaks cook up fast, so watch 'em!! Serve with wild rice or potatoes and a light salad.

Dave Buckley
Shreveport, Louisiana

RABBIT NUGGETS

2 lbs. rabbit breasts
2 cups flour
1 cup buttermilk
1 T. parsley
1 tsp. dried mustard
1 tsp. salt
1 tsp. garlic powder
1 tsp. pepper
2 cups vegetable oil or shortening

Cut the rabbit breast into 1 inch strips. In a bowl, mix flour, buttermilk, parsley, mustard, salt, garlic powder, pepper; stir batter until smooth.

Heat oil in skillet to about 410°, making sure it doesn't smoke. Dip the rabbit breasts into batter, then place in hot oil. Fry about 12 minutes or until rabbit is golden brown and crispy.

Teresa Nolan
Sault Ste. Marie, Michigan

DEVILED RABBIT OR SQUIRREL

1 rabbit or squirrel, cut into serving-size pieces	1 cup hot water
salt and pepper, to taste	2 tsp. Worcestershire sauce
1 tsp. paprika	2 tsp. ketchup
2 T. flour	1½ tsp. dry mustard
½ cup shortening	

Sprinkle salt, pepper and paprika on meat; roll in flour. Brown well in shortening and remove from pan. Add remaining flour to shortening in pan and stir until smooth. Add water, Worcestershire, ketchup and mustard, mixing well. Put meat in casserole dish and pour the sauce over. Cover and bake at 350° for 1 to 1½ hours or until tender, in 350° oven.

Al Jenewein
North Freedom, Wisconsin

SQUIRREL SAUTÉ

4 squirrels, cut up	½ cup pimiento-stuffed green olives, drained
¼ cup olive oil	salt and pepper to taste
1 cup garlic-and-herb spaghetti sauce or your own pasta sauce	4 cups chopped fresh Swiss chard, or 2 12-oz. pkgs. frozen Swiss chard or spinach, drained
1 cup water	
1 6-oz. can pitted black olives drained	

Heat oil over medium-high heat in large frying pan; add squirrel and brown. Add remaining ingredients except seasoning and Swiss chard. Simmer for 1 hour, add salt and pepper to taste.

Cover and simmer for 3-4 hours until squirrel is done. Add additional water as necessary to keep fluid in bottom of pan. Remove any pieces of squirrel that are cooked more quickly than others. When meat is done, return all pieces to pan. Stir in chard; cover and cook for 10 minutes. Serve over your favorite pasta.

Robert Samson
Powell, Missouri

RABBIT CASSEROLE

1 large rabbit, dressed
8 slices of bacon
2 small onions, sliced
2 medium potatoes, sliced
2 cups hot water
1 tsp. salt
1/4 tsp. pepper
1/2 tsp. dried basil
  flour

Cut up rabbit. Fry the bacon until light brown. Arrange bacon and rabbit in a deep casserole dish. Top with onions and potatoes. Add water, salt, pepper and basil to dish. Sprinkle lightly with flour. Cover and bake at 325° for 2 hours.

Jerry Buzard
Brookville, Pennsylvania

SPICY BARBECUE RABBIT

2 medium rabbits, cut into pieces
1 cup barbecue sauce
1 tsp. cayenne pepper
1 tsp. Cajun spice
3-4 T. hot pepper sauce
1/2 tsp. black pepper
1/4 tsp. salt
1/2 gallon ice water

Combine sauces and spices in medium bowl and mix thoroughly. Dip rabbit in mixture to coat. Cook rabbit in smoker or in oven at 325° for about 1^{1}/2 hours, turning and basting with sauce as needed. The ice water is for when you start eating!

James E. Britt
Lexington, Indiana

REAL PORCUPINE MEATBALLS

1½ lbs. ground porcupine meat
½ cup uncooked rice
¼ cup chopped onion
1 clove garlic, minced
   salt and pepper
   pinch of dried oregano
1 can tomato soup
½ can beef bouillon

Combine all ingredients except soup and bouillon. Shape into small balls and place in 9x13 inch casserole. Mix soup and bouillon in saucepan and bring to simmer (or heat in microwave 4 minutes.) Pour over meatballs, and bake at 350° for 35-40 minutes. Serve with sourdough biscuits and steamed, buttered carrots.

Andi Flanagan
Kodiak, Alaska

BUNNY ADOBO

1 rabbit, approx. 3-4 lbs., cut into pieces
1 lb. small mushrooms
½ cup soy sauce
½ cup red wine vinegar
4 cloves garlic, minced
2 bay leaves
1 T. crushed black peppercorns
1 cup olive oil
3 T. chili pepper powder (not cayenne, too hot!)

In a large stewpot, combine all ingredients. Bring to a boil. Reduce heat, and simmer, stirring occasionally, for 1 hour or until meat is almost falling off the bone. Serve over plenty of hot steamed rice. Good with cool cucumber salad and cold beer.

Andi Flanagan
Kodiak, Alaska

ANDI'S TOP-SECRET SLOW-COOKER RABBIT TERIYAKI

1	3-4 lb. rabbit, cut into pieces	1/4	cup sherry
3	T. shortening	3	cloves garlic, minced
1	can chicken broth	1	T. sesame oil
1 1/2	cups brown sugar	1/2	tsp. ground ginger
1	cup soy sauce	1	bunch green onions
1/4	cup ketchup	3	papayas
		6	cups cooked white rice

This dish has won me acclaim from Nome to Ketchikan — and this is the first time I have ever revealed the recipe!

In a large skillet, brown rabbit well in the shortening; don't crowd the pan. Add rabbit pieces to slow cooker as they are browned. Combine next 8 ingredients in saucepan. Slice white part of green onions, and add to saucepan. Bring to a boil, whisking to dissolve sugar. Pour over rabbit, and stir to coat. Let cook 12 hours or more, until meat falls off the bones. Cool and refrigerator overnight.

Remove rabbit meat from bones and return to sauce in slow cooker. Cook on low for about 6 hours. When ready to serve, peel, halve and seed papayas. Heat papayas in a low oven just until hot. Place each papaya half on a bed of hot, cooked rice and spoon teriyaki rabbit over all. Sprinkle with the chopped green onion tops.

Andi Flanagan
Kodiak, Alaska

RABBIT SCALLOPINI

    1   rabbit or grouse, cut up
    ½   cup sifted flour
    2   T. butter
    2   T. oil
    2   cups dry sherry or dry burgundy
    ½   cup chopped onion
    1   clove garlic
    1   tsp. salt
    ¼   tsp. each pepper, thyme, rosemary
          and oregano
    2   cups or more sliced
          fresh mushrooms

Dredge meat in flour. Turn electric fry pan to 420°, and brown meat quickly in butter and oil. Remove meat. Stir in remaining ingredients, except mushrooms. After 2 minutes, return meat to pan. Cover and cook at 225° for 30 minutes. Add more wine if necessary to keep moist. Add mushrooms; cook, covered for 15 minutes more. Serve with baked potatoes and a mild vegetable.

P. Glenn Armstrong
Tracy, California

SQUIRREL JAMBALAYA

4 squirrels, cleaned and quartered
6 strips bacon
2 T. bacon drippings
2 T. butter
1 medium onion, chopped
2 cloves garlic, peeled and finely chopped
1 medium green bell pepper, chopped
3 ribs celery, chopped
1 can beef consommé
1 cup water
1 can tomatoes with green chilies
1 small can tomato paste
1½ cups uncooked white rice
1 T. dried parsley
2 bay leaves
1 tsp. each basil, salt and thyme
½ tsp. each of black, cayenne and white pepper
½ tsp. chili powder

Place squirrels in a large pot and cover with water. Boil until meat is done; remove from heat. Allow to cool and then remove meat from bones; set aside.

In a large pot, fry the bacon strips until crisp. Remove from heat, crumble bacon and set aside. Pour off all but 2 tablespoons bacon drippings. Return pot to stove and add the butter. Melt butter over medium-low heat. Add all chopped vegetables; sauté for 5 minutes. Stir in beef consommé, water, tomatoes, tomato paste, crumbled bacon strips, rice and all seasonings. Bring to a boil and add the squirrel meat.

Cover pot and reduce heat to a simmer. Continue to simmer for 45 minutes, stirring occasionally. Add a little water and stir if jambalaya becomes too dry. Remove from heat and serve. Hot garlic bread adds a nice touch.

Ronald Perry
Alvin, Texas

SMOTHERED SQUIRREL IN ONION GRAVY

4 squirrels, cleaned and cut up
1 cup all-purpose flour
1½ tsp. salt
2 tsp. black pepper
¼ cup vegetable oil
2 cups water
2 large onions, chopped
1 medium green bell pepper, chopped
2 ribs celery, chopped
6 green onions, chopped
½ cup fresh mushrooms, chopped

Combine flour, salt and pepper. Roll squirrel pieces in flour mixture until well coated. Heat oil over medium heat in a large skillet or Dutch oven. Fry squirrel pieces in oil until golden brown. Remove squirrel and set aside.

Stir any remaining flour left from coating the squirrel pieces into hot vegetable oil. Add the water and mix well. Allow the mixture to simmer over low heat for 10 minutes, stirring occasionally. Add all chopped vegetables, and mix well. Sauté vegetables over low heat for 10-12 minutes, or until soft. Add fried squirrel pieces and cover.

Simmer over low heat for 1½ hours. Stirring occasionally and adding water if gravy becomes too thick. Adjust seasonings, if necessary. Serve over cooked rice or cooked noodles.

Ronald Perry
Alvin, Texas

APRICOT RABBIT

    2   small rabbits, cut into pieces
    1   8-oz. bottle creamy Russian dressing
    1   cup apricot jam
  1/4   cup apricot brandy
    1   pkg. dry onion soup mix

Place rabbit in a single layer in baking dish. Mix all remaining ingredients and pour over rabbit. Bake at 350° for 1 hour, basting every 15 minutes, until meat is tender.

Arthur McClearn
Cresson, Pennsylvania

SQUIRREL PATTIES

    5   squirrels
    6   slices of bread, crumbled
    1   large onion, chopped
    1   cup water
    1   cup beer
    1   cup flour
  2-3   eggs, beaten
    1   cup chopped mushrooms
  1/4   cup lemon juice
 2 1/2 T. bacon bits
 2 1/2 tsp. salt
    1   tsp. pepper
        oil for frying

Clean and cut squirrels into bite-size pieces; boil in water for 1½ hours. Grind cooked meat and place in bowl. Add remaining ingredients, except oil, and mix well by hand. Form mixture into patties. Fry patties in skillet in hot oil to desired doneness.

James D. Deffibaugh
Osterburg, Pennsylvania

Squirrel Jerky

Any meat may be used: squirrel, pheasant, duck or just about any low-fat meat.

squirrel meat or other low-fat meat
2-4 cups water
2 cups soy sauce
½ cup Worcestershire sauce
1 pkg. meat marinade
2 T. liquid smoke
½ T. black pepper
½ T. garlic salt
10 drops hot pepper sauce
sprinkle of crushed red pepper flakes

Cut meat into strips ⅛-¼ inch thick, cutting across the grain for tender jerky or with the grain for chewy texture. Combine remaining ingredients. Add meat and stir; refrigerate for 24 hours.

Remove meat from marinade and put directly into dehydrator. Dry at 145° for 12 hours. When meat is partially dried, extra Worcestershire sauce, steak sauce or barbecue sauce may be sprinkled on for extra taste. Store jerky in jar with lid for short-term storage or in plastic bags in freezer for long-term storage.

Laverne C. Wubben
Hazel Green, Wisconsin

BEER-BRAISED RABBIT

1	2 ½-3 lb. rabbit, dressed
2	T. canola oil
4	medium potatoes, quartered
4	medium carrots, cut into half-inch pieces
1	medium onion, coarsely chopped
1	can beer, or 1½ cups apple cider (or juice)
¼	cup chili sauce
½	tsp. salt
¼	cup cold water
2	T. all-purpose flour

If desired, sprinkle rabbit with salt and pepper. In a 12 inch skillet, brown rabbit on all sides in hot oil. Drain fat. Add potatoes, carrots, and onion to skillet. Combine beer, chili sauce, and salt. Pour over rabbit and vegetables in skillet. Bring to boil; reduce heat. Cover and simmer for 35-45 minutes.

Remove rabbit and vegetables from skillet. Keep warm. Skim fat from pan juices. Return juice mixture to skillet. Combine water and flour with juices in skillet. Cook until thick, stirring constantly, and serve with rabbit and vegetables.

Robert Fout,
Berea, Kentucky

Rabbit Stew

3	rabbits, boned and cubed
	Worcestershire sauce
	garlic salt
2	T. butter or margarine
2	cans of beef broth
1/2	tsp. pepper
1	tsp. dried oregano
1	tsp. dried summer savory
1	tsp. ground cumin
1	tsp. dried thyme
1/2	tsp. dried sage
1/2	tsp. dried tarragon
1	large onion
2	celery stalks
3	potatoes
3-4	carrots
1	10-oz, pkg, frozen peas
1/2	cup hearty burgundy wine or water
1/4	cup all-purpose flour

Scott D. Swank

In a large frying pan, brown meat in butter sprinkled liberally with garlic salt, Worcestershire sauce. Cook until well browned and sauce is boiled away. Set aside.

In a large pot, combine beef broth and seasonings. Cover and bring to a boil. Cut vegetables into pieces and add to broth. Add peas and meat. Add water to cover. Reduce heat and cook until vegetables are tender and liquid is at desired level, about 4 hours. Stir flour into wine until smooth. Stir flour/wine mixture into stew. Simmer until thickened.

Scott D. Swank
Bel Air, Maryland

MAINE JUGGED HARE

2 rabbits, cut into serving pieces
1 T. vinegar
1 T. salt
1 cup flour
    olive oil
2-3 cups mushrooms
2 medium onions, quartered
1/8 tsp. ground cloves
1 tsp. salt
1/2 tsp. pepper
2 garlic cloves, minced (or use garlic powder)
    chicken broth to cover meat

Place rabbit pieces in water to cover and add 1 tablespoon vinegar and 1 tablespoon salt; soak for 1 hour. Drain and place in bag with flour, shaking to coat. Over medium heat, brown rabbit in olive oil. Place rabbit in bean pot, layering with mushrooms and onions. Add cloves, salt, pepper and garlic. Heat chicken broth and add to pot.

Cover pot, and bake at 275° for 3-4 hours. Just before serving, place rabbit pieces on serving platter. Pour liquid from pot into saucepan and bring to a boil. Remove from heat. Add paste made from 3 tablespoons flour and water; stir until smooth. Heat again until thickened. Pour gravy over rabbit.

Warren Leask
Wiscasset, Maine

GAME BIRDS

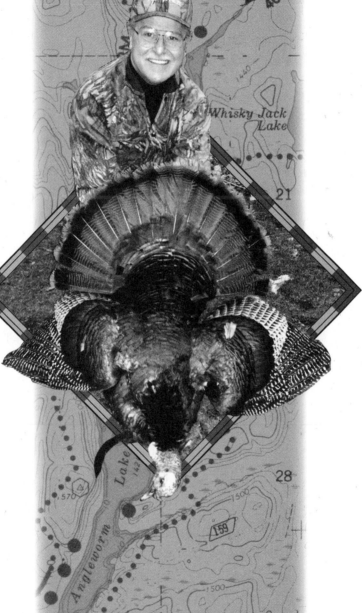

PHEASANT IN SOUR CREAM SAUCE

2 pheasants, 1³/₄ lbs. each
1 cup flour
¹/₂ cup vegetable oil
   salt and pepper
2 T. flour
2 T. butter
1 cup heavy cream
1 cup milk
2 cups water
2 tsp. chicken base or bouillon granules
¹/₄ tsp. white pepper
¹/₂ tsp. garlic powder
¹/₂ cup sour cream

Cut each pheasants into 8 pieces, splitting each breast. Dust pieces of pheasant in 1 cup flour; sauté in frying pan with oil until golden brown. Remove to a roasting pan; sprinkle with salt and pepper. Set aside.

To prepare roux, place 2 tablespoons butter and 2 tablespoons flour in small, heavy bottomed pan over low heat; cook, stirring, for several minutes. (The cooking removes the pasty taste of the flour.) Add cream, milk and water to saucepan. Add chicken base, pepper and garlic powder. Cook, stirring constantly, until mixture thickens.

Add the sour cream to mixture and stir until smooth. Pour sauce over pheasants in roasting pan. Cover and bake at 325° for 2 hours or until pheasant is tender. Serve sour cream sauce with fowl. Wild rice is an excellent accompanying dish with this.

Robert Czaplinski
Stevens Point, Wisconsin

SUNSHINE STUFFED GROUSE

2-3   grouse, dressed
1½   T. chopped onion
1½   T. chopped celery
  2   T. butter
  2   cups dried bread cubes
  ¼   tsp. salt
  ¼   tsp. pepper
  ¼   tsp. poultry seasoning
  1   cup orange juice

Cook onions and celery in butter until tender. Remove from heat. Stir in bread cubes, seasonings and enough orange juice to moisten. Stuff mixture into cavities of grouse.

Place stuffed grouse in foil-lined, roasting pan. Bake covered at 375° for 1½ hours. Uncover for last ½ hour, and baste frequently with remaining orange juice.

S. Wesley Waldron
Trout Run, Pennsylvania

GREELY GROUSE

  4   grouse breasts
  1   onion, chopped
  1   cup sliced fresh mushrooms
  1   green bell pepper, chopped
  1   cup sour cream
  2   cans cream of mushroom soup

Cut breast meat into chunks and brown in a frying pan. Add onion, mushrooms and green pepper; sauté until tender-crisp. Mix sour cream and cream of mushroom soup in a bowl. Stir soup mixture into skillet. Cover and simmer for 1 hour. Serve over rice, potatoes, noodles or toast. Works well with dove, quail, etc.

Christopher R. Prima
Ft. Rucker, Alabama

Pot Pie

       breast of grouse or pheasant
1   medium onion, diced
       poultry seasoning
1   tsp. margarine
1   pkg. ready-made 2-crust pie crust
1   can cream of celery soup
¼   cup milk
1   can mixed vegetables, drained

Cut breast into small pieces. Sprinkle onion with poultry seasoning.
Brown breast and onion in 1 teaspoon margarine. Place bottom of
ready-made pie crust into greased pie plate. Mix celery soup, milk and
mixed vegetables. Pour soup mixture, grouse and onion into pie shell.
Put on top crust, trimming and pinching edges together. Make several
slits on top. Bake at 350° for 50 minutes or until brown.

Gary L. Rupert
Avonmore, Pennsylvania

Scalloped Wild Turkey

4   cups cubed cooked wild turkey
6   slices bread, torn into small pieces
2   eggs, beaten
1   can cream of mushroom soup
1   can chicken noodle soup
4   T. butter
2   cups crushed corn flakes

Combine turkey, bread, eggs and soups; pour into 10 inch baking dish.
Melt butter and toss with crushed corn flakes; sprinkle over top of
turkey. Bake, covered, 45 minutes. Uncover and bake 15 minutes more.

Bill Wanpler
Lancaster, Ohio

OLD FASHIONED PHEASANT

pheasant(s), dressed and cut up
bacon strips, about 6 per bird
flour
heavy cream or milk
salt and pepper to taste

In a skillet, cook bacon strips until crisp; remove to drain. On high heat, sear pheasant pieces in bacon grease on each side for about 15 seconds. Reduce heat to simmer, cover skillet, and cook 20-30 minutes. Remove pheasant pieces.

Add flour, cream, salt and pepper to remaining grease, stirring vigorously; serve mixture as gravy. Serve pheasant with rice, potatoes, or carrots. Variation (the lush Latvian): After searing pheasant, add some chardonnay or chablis according to taste during the simmering.

T. Sulmeisters
Torrington, Wyoming

BAKED GROUSE

1 grouse, dressed
3 slices bacon
3 orange slices
1/4 cup melted butter
2 T. orange juice
2 T. honey
   grated orange peel

Place grouse in roasting pan. Cover with sliced bacon and orange slices. Mix remaining ingredients for basting sauce. Bake at 400°, covered, for 20-30 minutes or until tender, basting frequently with sauce.

Roy B. Lehman
North Platte, NE

BARBECUED QUAIL (GAMBEL, CALIFORNIA, OR BOBWHITE)

12 whole quail breasts
24 quail legs
    butter
    lemon
1 pkg. wild rice blend

1 can diced green
    chilies
12 bacon strips
    bay leaves

Boil breasts and legs in water until partially cooked. Brown legs in butter and a squeeze of lemon until seared; set aside and keep warm. Prepare rice and set aside. Place a spoonful of chilies in cavity of each breast; wrap breast in one strip of bacon. Place each breast on individual pieces of foil; top each with a squeeze of lemon, a pat of butter and one bay leaf. Wrap tightly. Cook 12 quail packets on hot barbecue for 10-15 minutes, or until breast is thoroughly cooked. Serve foil packets with rice and fried legs.

Mr. and Mrs. Ed Bartels
Lake Havasu City, Arizona

MEXICAN PHEASANT

2 cups cooked pheasant, cut into 1" bites
1 can cream of mushroom soup
1 can cream of chicken soup
1 onion, finely chopped
1¹/₃ cups medium salsa
1 cup sour cream
1 cup Cheddar cheese, grated
1 cup Monterey Jack cheese, grated
1 pkg. flour tortillas, cut into 1-inch strips

Combine pheasant, soups, onion, salsa, sour cream and 1½ cups mixed cheeses in baking dish, layer mixture with tortilla strips, 2-3 times starting with tortilla on bottom. Top with remaining cheeses. Bake at 350° for 30 minutes, or until cheese is bubbly.

Don Kuhlmann
Winona, Minnesota

WILD PHEASANT A L'ORANGE

2 small pheasants or 1 large pheasant, quartered
1 6-oz. can frozen orange juice, thawed
1/2 cup water
1/4 tsp. ground cinnamon
1/4 tsp. ground cloves
1 tsp. salt

Place pheasant pieces skin side up in slow cooker. Combine remaining ingredients and pour over pheasant. Cover and cook on low for 7-8 hours. Reserve liquid for gravy. Serve over rice.

Al Jenewein
North Freedom, Wisconsin

SHARON'S DOVE BREAST

24 dove breasts
1/2 cup baking soda
3-4 T. salt
   fat-free Italian dressing
   Creole seasoning
   garlic pepper to taste

Thoroughly wash dove breasts; cover with water and add baking soda and salt. Cover and refrigerate for 2-4 hours, stirring once or twice. Wash breasts and drain.

Pour dressing over breasts and sprinkle with Creole seasoning and garlic-pepper. Mix, cover and refrigerate 2-4 hours, stirring a couple of times.

Grill breasts over medium heat, skin side up, for about 20minutes, turning in last few minutes to brown sides. Baste during cooking with fresh Italian dressing.

J. Larry Locke
Bryan, Texas

TURKEY TENDERS

½   turkey breast, cut into 1" cubes
¼   cup light soy sauce
4   T. lemon juice
1   cup flour
½   cup bread crumbs
¼   tsp. salt
¼   tsp. black pepper
¼   tsp. garlic pepper
½   tsp. dried parsley
½   tsp. dried basil
½   tsp. sesame seeds
    oil for deep frying

Marinate turkey cubes in soy sauce and lemon juice in a covered dish in the refrigerator for 2 hours. Drain the marinade. Mix remaining ingredients, except oil; roll cubes in flour mixture to coat. Set aside. Heat oil in deep fryer. Deep fry the turkey tenders to a light golden brown. Avoid overcooking to prevent drying the meat as wild turkey breast has minimal fat.

Socorro Heft
Sonora, Texas

PHEASANT SALAD

- 1 pheasant, dressed
- 2 bunches green onions, chopped
- 2 T. olive oil
- 1 T. soy sauce

Heat 1 gallon of water to a boil; add pheasant, return to boil, remove from heat, and let sit for 1 hour. Pick meat from carcass and cut into bite-size pieces. Mix meat with onions. Heat olive oil until very hot. Add oil and soy sauce to turkey; toss to coat. Cool before serving.

Richard Flick
Denmark, Wisconsin

ROASTED RINGNECKS

- 2 pheasants, dressed
- 1 can chicken noodle soup
- 4 cups white wine
- 1½ chicken broth
- 1 cup onion, chopped
- 8 cloves of garlic, crushed
- 1 tsp. lemon-garlic seasoning
- ½ tsp. ground ginger
- ¼ tsp. garlic powder
- 1 tsp. poultry seasoning

Put pheasants in large roasting pan; and pour chicken noodle soup over birds. Pour wine and chicken broth into pan, but not over birds. Sprinkle onion and garlic around birds. Sprinkle lemon-garlic seasoning, ginger, garlic powder and poultry seasoning over birds. Cover and roast at 250° for 4 hours, basting every ¹/₂ hour.

Dave Lanigan
Grove City, Pennsylvania

MIKE'S PHEASANT SOUP

 1   pheasant carcass
12   cups water
 2   bay leaves
 8   peppercorns
 1   onion, chopped
 3   carrots, chopped
 3   stalks celery, chopped
1-2   cups cooked, diced pheasant meat,
 2   cups diced mushrooms
     salt and pepper
 1   T. dried marjoram
 1   T. dried parsley
 1   T. minced chives
½   cup dry sherry
1-2   cups uncooked macaroni

Simmer carcass, bay leaves and peppercorns in 12 cups water for
approximately 45 minutes. Strain broth and discard carcass and spices.
Add remaining ingredients, except sherry to broth. Simmer for
45 minutes, or until vegetables are tender. Stir in macaroni; simmer
for 20 minutes, or until tender.

Mike S. Vinzinski
Wilmington, Delaware

DOVES IN CORNBREAD STUFFING

24 dove breasts, bone-in
6 T. butter
1 large shallot, finely chopped
2 T. bacon drippings
2 T. dried parsley
2 boxes cornbread stuffing

Melt 2 tablespoons butter in a large nonstick skillet; add shallots. Cook until lightly brown. Add the bacon drippings to the pan When drippings are melted, add the dove breasts and parsley; stir until breasts are browned on all sides.

Mix and cook the stuffing according to the box instructions. Divide stuffing into two equal amounts; placing the first half into a large Dutch oven. Layer breasts in pan and top with remaining stuffing. Cover and bake at 375° for 45 minutes.

Mike Crampton
Bowie, Maryland

KEITH'S PHEASANT SOUP

¼ cup margarine
1 cup finely diced onion
1 cup finely diced celery
1 cup finely diced carrots
⅓ cup flour
8 cups chicken broth*
⅓ cup finely diced green pepper
⅓ cup finely diced red pepper
1 cup cooked wild rice,
1 cup cooked diced pheasant
1 bay leaf
1 cup half-and-half warmed
    salt and pepper to taste

Heat margarine in a large saucepan. Add onion, celery and carrots and cook over low heat until tender, stirring occasionally. Add flour and cook for 5 minutes, stirring constantly. (Do not brown.) Gradually stir in chicken broth until blended.

Bring to a boil, cover and cook over low heat for 5 minutes. Add green pepper, red pepper, wild rice, pheasant and bay leaf; heat another 5 minutes. Stir in half-and-half and heat but do not boil. Season to taste with salt and pepper. Discard bay leaf before serving.

*Instead of 8 cups chicken broth, use 3 cans of chicken broth, 2 cups of water and 3 chicken bouillon cubes.

Keith Moen
Thief River Falls, Minnesota

PHEASANT FEAST

3-4 pheasants, dressed
1 medium yellow onion, peeled and chopped
½ green bell pepper, chopped
3 ribs of celery, chopped
1 can chicken broth (or 2 cups)
2 T. butter or margarine
½ tsp. dried rosemary
2 T. lemon juice
1 cup heavy cream
1 T. minced parsley
⅓ cup unsifted flour
⅓ cup milk

Place pheasant in large kettle of water. Boil on low until meat comes off the bones easily. Remove meat from bones and chop into bite-size pieces. Set aside.

In clean kettle, combine remaining ingredients, except flour and milk. Heat on low until creamy, and celery, onion and pepper are tender. Blend flour and milk together; add to mixture. Cook, stirring constantly, until liquid thickens. Add chopped pheasant. Serve over egg noodles with biscuits on the side.

Kyle Slabik
Spring City, PA

Dove Breast Paté

Great as a cracker spread, hors d'ouevres or sandwich filler.

- 12 dove breasts
- 2 cloves garlic, sliced thin
- 1/2 white onion, diced
- 4 green onions, sliced in 1/4" pieces
- 1/2 bay leaf
- 1 tsp. finely chopped cilantro
- 1/2 tsp. salt
- 1/4 tsp. black pepper, fresh cracked
- 1/4 tsp. dried oregano
- 2 slices bacon, diced
- 1/4 tsp. Worcestershire sauce
- 1 T. olive oil
- 1 T. butter

Place dove breasts in eight cups of water in a saucepan, and bring to a boil. Reduce to a simmer and put in remaining ingredients, except olive oil and butter. Cook for 30 minutes or until dove meat is well done. Set aside to cool.

When cool, pour contents of pan into colander; remove dove breasts. Remove meat from breastbones, and grind or finely chop meat. Place ingredients remaining in colander into skillet with olive oil and butter. Stir constantly over medium heat until bacon is crisp; remove from heat.

Place all ingredients into a blender; blend well. Spoon mixture into a paté or gelatin mold. Pack mixture tightly, cover with plastic wrap, and place some weight on it, like a saucer on which a container of water is placed. Refrigerate until ready to use. Does not freeze well so don't make more than you will use.

Henry L. Homrighaus, Jr.
Kennedy, Texas

PHEASANT A LA PARISIENNE

4 breasts pheasants, or thighs and breasts from
2 pheasants
1 chicken bouillon cube
1 cup boiling water
1 can cream of mushroom soup
1 can cream of celery soup
1/4 cup crumbled bleu cheese (may substitute parmesan)

Place pheasant in a covered casserole dish or Dutch oven. Dissolve
1 chicken bouillon cube in boiling water. Combine both cans of soup and
bouillon in a bowl and pour over pheasant. Cover and bake at 350° for
1 hour. Remove pheasant from oven and uncover. Sprinkle cheese over
top of pheasant and return to oven uncovered. Broil at 400° for
5 minutes. Serve with wild rice and green beans almondine.

This can be cooked over a campfire with the coals arranged in a ring
around the outside of a cast iron Dutch oven. During the last 5 minutes
of cooking, add the cheese and cover.

William C. Meyer
Sandwich, Illinois

PHEASANT OH YES!

1 pheasant, quartered
1 can condensed cream
of chicken soup
1/2 cup apple cider
1 1/2 T. Worcestershire
3/4 tsp. salt
1/3 cup chopped onion
1 clove minced garlic
1 small can sliced
mushrooms, drained
paprika

Place pheasant in ungreased 9x9x2-inch baking dish. Mix soup, cider,
Worcestershire sauce, salt, onion, garlic and mushrooms. Pour over
pheasant. Sprinkle generously with paprika. Bake at 350° for 1 1/2-2
hours, basting occasionally. After 1 hour, sprinkle again with paprika.

Dale Overbeek
West Olive, Michigan

PTARMIGAN BREASTS IN SOUR CREAM

4 ptarmigan breasts, boneless
1 cup fine, dry bread crumbs
   seasoned salt and black pepper
1/4 tsp. finely ground rosemary
2 eggs, beaten with 1/4 cup melted butter
3 T. butter
2 cups sour cream
3 T. white wine
3 T. finely minced onion
2 cloves garlic, minced
   paprika

Mix the bread crumbs with the seasoned salt, pepper and rosemary.
Dip the breasts in the egg/butter mixture, then roll in the crumbs. In
a flame-proof casserole, brown the breasts in the 3 tablespoons butter.
Mix the sour cream with the onion, wine and garlic; cover the breasts
with mixture. Generously sprinkle with paprika. Cover, and bake at 350°
for 45 minutes to 1 hour, or until fork tender. Serve with wild rice and
candied carrots.

Andi Flanagan
Kodiak, Alaska

FRESH GROUSE AND STUFFING

1 grouse, dressed
⅓ cup chopped white onion
1 small clove garlic, chopped
3 T. butter or margarine
1 8-oz. can mushrooms
2 cups dry bread crumbs
1 egg, beaten
   sage to taste, crushed or broken
   dry tarragon, small dusting to taste
   salt and pepper to taste
½ cup melted butter or margarine
   onion powder

To make stuffing, quickly sauté onion and garlic in 3 tablespoons butter for a few minutes, taking care not to overcook; keep onion firm. Drain mushrooms, reserving liquid. In a large bowl, combine mushrooms, bread crumbs, sautéed onions and remaining ingredients, except melted butter and onion powder. Mix well with hands, thoroughly combining all ingredients, until stuffing is moist enough to form a moist ball; use reserved liquid from mushrooms to add moisture as necessary.

Stuff bird; any extra stuffing not used in the bird can be baked in an uncovered casserole dish along with the bird. Place bird, breast-up, in a shallow 8x10-inch pan. Brush entire bird with melted butter and sprinkle lightly with onion powder, salt and pepper to taste. Bake at 325° for 30-35 minutes per pound, or until leg joint moves easily or breast meat begins to pull away from breast bone at top. Periodically brush entire bird with melted butter during baking to keep meat moist.

Vincent M. Boreczky
Fennville, Michigan

Grouse Fajitas

This whole meal takes only about fifteen minutes to prepare and will make you the hero of the camp! Other game birds may be substituted.

　4　grouse, boned
　　　peanut oil or stir-fry oil
　1　large sweet onion, chopped
　1　clove garlic, minced
　1　can Spam, cubed
　½　cup water
　　　tortillas, pita or pocket bread
　1　ripe avocado, sliced
　　　salsa (optional)

Heat peanut oil in skillet. Add onion and garlic, and sauté until onion becomes slightly clear. Remove from skillet and set aside. Brown Spam in skillet until very brown; place Spam with onion. Brown boned grouse in same skillet peanut oil, then add onion and Spam to the grouse. Add water, cover pan, reduce heat and let simmer until all meat is done.

Spoon fajita mixture on a tortilla and add strips of avocado and salsa to taste; roll up tortilla and eat while hot.

D.L. McCartney
Kennedale, Texas

PHEASANT YAKATORI

1 lb. boned pheasant breast
1/3 cup soy sauce
3 T. dry sherry
1 tsp. sugar
2 cloves garlic
1/2 tsp. minced ginger

In a large bowl, combine soy sauce, sherry, sugar, garlic and ginger to make marinade. Cut pheasant breast into bite-size pieces and place in marinade for 30 minutes. Heat broiler. Breast pieces may be placed on skewers or arranged on broiler pan. Broil approximately 7 minutes or until done to taste.

P. Glenn Armstrong
Tracy, California

SMOKY TURKEY BREAST

1 5-lb. turkey breast
1/3 cup soy sauce
1/2 cup dry sherry

1 tsp. grated ginger
1 tsp. liquid smoke

Rinse breast and remove any excess fat. Combine soy sauce, sherry, ginger and liquid smoke in plastic food storage bag. Place turkey into bag and squeeze out as much air as possible and seal bag. Place bag in bowl and refrigerate 24 hours, turning occasionally.

To cook, remove turkey from bag and place skin side down in 4-quart microwave-safe dish with lid. Add marinade from bag. Cover and microwave on high for 25 minutes. Turn turkey over and microwave at 70% power (medium-high) for 20 minutes, rotating dish twice. Check internal doneness with instant reading thermometer or use temperature probe on microwave; breasts are done when temperature reaches 165°.

Let stand, covered, for 15 minutes to finish cooking. Serve thinly sliced with some of the drippings in the casserole spooned over the slices.

P. Glenn Armstrong
Tracy, California

FRUITY PHEASANT

This can also be made with quail, chukar, or for that matter, chicken, as easily as with pheasant. I suggest you use at least 6 quail breasts if you intend to serve 2 people.

    2   boneless, skinned pheasant breasts
    1   lemon
    2   T. butter
        chopped parsley
    4   peach or pear halves
    1/4 cup plain yogurt
    1/4 cup sour cream
        fresh mint leaves (optional)
        slivered almonds (optional)

Place breasts on foil in a baking pan and put a squeeze of lemon juice and a pat of butter on each breast. Sprinkle with parsley and place peach halves evenly on breasts. Wrap up tightly in foil and bake at 325° for 35 minutes. Mix yogurt and sour cream together. Add mint leaves and almonds. and stir until smooth; sauce should be room temperature. When pheasant is done, slice meat and place on plates with the cooked peaches. Add sauce and serve. I like this served on a bed of rice or wilted greens.

Keith Baker
Falls Church, Virginia

HAWAIIAN DOVE RUMAKI

12 dove breasts
1½ cups soy sauce
¼ cup brown sugar
¼ cup dry red or white wine
1 T. sesame oil
⅓ cup crushed pineapple, undrained
2 T. sesame seeds
1 clove garlic, crushed
1 can sliced water chestnuts
12 slices bacon

Combine soy sauce, sugar, wine, oil, pineapple and sesame seeds in a quart-size plastic bag; shake to mix. Starting at the top of the breast bone, fillet each dove breast from the breast bone making 24 boneless breast medallions. Place the water chestnuts and filleted dove breasts in plastic bag and refrigerate 2-4 hours, turning occasionally.

Preheat grill to medium hot. Cut each piece of bacon in half. Remove the water chestnuts and dove breasts from the marinade. Sandwich each dove breast medallion between two slices of water chestnut; wrap with a piece of bacon, overlapping the bacon ends and securing with a toothpick. Place in a cooking basket and place on the grill. Grill 5-10 minutes, turning occasionally.

David Hoskins
Panama City, Florida

QUAIL A LA VOLLMAR
GLAZED QUAIL WITH PECANS AND MARMALADE

4-6 quail, dressed
5 T. flour
1 pinch poultry seasoning
1 pinch ground black pepper
1 pinch onion salt
2 eggs, beaten
½ cup milk
1 cup ground pecans
¼ cup bread crumbs or crushed soda crackers
2-3 T. butter
½ orange
½ lemon
1 small can chicken broth
¼ cup marmalade
1 T. cornstarch

Wash quail well and leave slightly damp. Place quail in bag with flour that has been seasoned with poultry seasoning, black pepper, and onion salt; shake well and remove. Make egg wash by beating eggs, and milk together until well mixed. Dip quail into egg wash, then roll in ¾ cup pecans mixed well with ¼ cup bread crumbs.

Melt 2-3 tablespoons butter in a skillet and sauté quail in melted butter. After turning once, squeeze ½ orange and ½ lemon over quail. After browning, add 1 cup chicken broth mixed with ¼ cup marmalade. When quail are almost done, remove from skillet and keep warm. Dissolve cornstarch in ¼ cup remaining chicken broth; add to remaining butter and chicken broth stirring until thickented. Pour sauce over quail. Place in covered dish and bake at 350° for 10-15 minutes, until done. Remove, sprinkle with remaining ¼ cup pecans and garnish with chopped parsley. Use remaining sauce in pan for gravy.

Joseph E. Vollmar, Jr.
St. Louis, Missouri

BEER BATTER DOVE HORS D'OEUVRES

This recipe is for a dove appetizer for four people, to be served hot with drinks before dinner.

10	dove breasts, deboned (20 boneless medallions)
	Italian dressing
2	cups flour
1	tsp. baking powder
1	tsp. salt
	fresh beer (as needed; use enough beer to make batter semi-thick)
2	T. paprika
1/2	tsp. pepper

Rinse dove breasts well, drain and dry on clean towel. Put meat in a medium bowl and cover with a good brand of Italian dressing. Use a big spoon to turn dove meat so dressing and meat are well mixed. Marinate in refrigerator for 2-3 hours.

Mix remaining ingredients to make batter, adding beer in small amounts, beating well to achieve proper consistency; add beer as needed to make batter semi-thick. Let stand 10 minutes before using, then dredge dove meat through batter and deep fry until golden brown. (Use deep fryer and make sure the oil is very hot.) Cook in small quantities so as not to cool the oil too much. Cooking time is surprisingly short, so experiment with one or two pieces. Do not overcook! Doves are deliciously tender when flesh is mild pink. They are tough if overcooked.

Joseph E. Vollmar, Jr.
St. Louis, Missouri

Turkey with Orange Sauce

1	10 lb. wild turkey, dressed	¼	tsp. dried rosemary leaves
3	oranges, unpeeled	⅔	cup dry white wine
1	large onion	½	cup butter, melted
2	T. olive oil	1	clove garlic, minced
	salt and pepper	1	chicken bouillon cube
¼	tsp. dried oregano		

Dice one unpeeled orange, and onion; mix in bowl with olive oil, salt, pepper, oregano and rosemary. Fill cavity of bird with this mixture and roast at 325° until bird is done. Baste turkey while roasting with mixture made by combining wine, melted butter, juice from remaining two oranges, garlic, bouillon cube, and salt and pepper to taste. Heat mixture to dissolve bouillon. Discard stuffing before serving.

Arthur McClearn
Cresson, Pennsylvania

Grouse or Pheasant Corn Chowder

2   cups grouse or pheasant, diced into 1-inch chunks
¼   cup chopped onion
¼   cup chopped green pepper
2   T. butter
1   can condensed Cheddar cheese soup
1   soup can of milk
1   can creamed corn
1   strip bacon, fried and crumbled

Sauté the grouse in a saucepan with the onion, green pepper and butter until is cooked. Then add the cheese soup, milk, creamed corn and bacon. Simmer (do not boil) for 5 minutes, stirring frequently. Remove from the heat and serve with a crusty bread.

J. Nelson
River Falls, Wisconsin

TAMMY'S TURKEY SOUP

    2   cups chopped cooked turkey
    8   cups water, or half broth and half water
    1   cup uncooked white rice
    2   small to medium onions, chopped
  5-6   carrots, sliced
    1   pkg. onion soup mix
  1/2   cup chopped celery, or 1 tsp. celery seed
    4   beef bouillon cubes
    1   tsp. garlic powder
        pepper to taste
    1   large can stewed tomatoes

Combine all ingredients except the tomatoes in large pot. Simmer until vegetables are tender and rice is done, then add stewed tomatoes. Heat through and serve.

Daniel L. Parsons
Unity Township, Maine

SANDHILL CRANE AND BROCCOLI

    1   sandhill crane breast, cut into bite-size chunks
    4   T. vegetable oil
    2   broccoli stalks, cut into bite-size chunks
    3   T. soy sauce
  1/4   cup water

Brown crane breast in 2 tablespoons of vegetable oil. Set aside. Sauté the broccoli in the remaining 2 tablespoons of oil. When broccoli is tender, add the cooked crane meat, soy sauce and water; sauté for about 5 minutes. Add other vegetable, such as onions or snow peas, with the broccoli, if desired.

Manuel De Leon
Austwell, Texas

CURRIED BREAST

4   pheasants, grouse, or your favorite game bird, halved, skinned, boned and cut into bite-size pieces

¼ cup flour

¼ cup butter or margarine, melted

½ cup finely chopped onion

¼ cup chopped celery

¼ cup chopped green bell peppers

¼ cup golden raisins

¾ cup chicken broth, or stock made from the bones and skin

1½ cups half-and-half

1 T. curry powder

1 cup sliced toasted almonds

¼ tsp. salt

⅛ tsp. pepper

2 cups cooked rice

Dredge the bird in flour, then brown in butter in a large skillet. Remove the bird, reserving the drippings in the skillet. Set the bird aside.

Sauté the onion, celery, green pepper and raisins in the reserved drippings until tender. Add the chicken broth. Cook, uncovered, over low heat for 5 minutes. Stir in half-and-half, curry powder, almonds, salt and pepper. Simmer, uncovered, for 10 minutes. Add the cooked rice and mix well.

William S. Richards
Silver Bay, Minnesota

Francis Brossart

PHEASANT PASTA ALFREDO

2	pheasant breasts
1/2	T. butter
1/2	cup unsalted butter
4	cups heavy cream
1/2	cup shredded fresh parmesan cheese
	salt
	pepper
	pasta noodles

Cut the pheasant into bite-size pieces and fry in butter until tender and done. Meanwhile, melt unsalted butter in a saucepan; add heavy cream and parmesan. Stir over low heat until smooth and hot, do not boil. Add salt and pepper. Stir in pheasant. Serve over your favorite pasta noodles.

Francis Brossart
Dickinson, North Dakota

WATERFOWL

Jack Dietle

ROYAL QUACKERS

2   mallard or other large duck breast halves
2   pieces turkey breast, sliced thin
    swiss cheese, cut into strips
1   egg, beaten
1/2 cup flour
1/2 cup Italian bread crumbs
    salt-free all-purpose seasoning

Clean and butterfly each duck breast half. Place between 2 sheets of wax paper and pound until thin. Put flour, bread crumbs, and egg in three separate bowls; set aside. Trim turkey slices to width of cheese strips. Lay out one duck breast half, place 1 turkey slice in center, and top with cheese and seasoning to taste. Roll turkey around cheese then wrap duck around this roll, sealing all edges. Coat roll with flour. Dip in egg, then roll in bread crumbs. Place in lightly greased dish. Bake at 350° for 30-35 minutes.

Jack Dietle
West Monroe, Louisiana

WILD DUCK APPETIZERS

2 duck breasts
¼ cup lemon juice
¼ cup soy sauce
2 T. teriyaki sauce
1 T. Worcestershire sauce
2 tsp. garlic powder
1 tsp. onion powder
1 tsp. seasoned salt
2 tsp. sesame seeds
12-14 strips bacon
pepper

Make marinade by mixing all ingredients, except duck, bacon and pepper. Cut duck into ½ inch cubes and marinate for 12-24 hours. Cut bacon into 2½ inch lengths and wrap each duck piece with piece of bacon, securing with toothpicks. Pepper both sides generously. Bake at 350° for 10-15 minutes, or until bacon is crispy. Serve hot or at room temperature.

Bruce Waggoner
Harrison Township ,Michigan

CROCKED GOOSE

1 skinned and filleted goose breast
1 can favorite cream soup (mushroom or
    celery, etc.)
1 onion, sliced

Clean, skin and fillet goose breast; soak in salt water. Put onion, breast and soup in slow cooker. Cook 8 hours on low. Serve over wild rice.

Eric Singley
Edwardsburg, Michigan

SAGE HEN SOUP

4-6 sage hen or duck legs
  1 cup elbow or shell macaroni or any type of pasta
     small amount of spaghetti broken into pieces
  1 small can sliced mushrooms
  1 14$\frac{1}{2}$-oz. can mixed vegetables
  3 14$\frac{1}{2}$-oz. cans beef broth
     garlic powder to taste
     seasoned salt and pepper to taste

Add 2 cans beef broth, seasonings and sage hen to pressure cooker; pressure cook for approx. 25 minutes. Meat should be very tender and fall from bone. Be sure to remove all the meat from the bones and return meat to broth in the pot. Add macaroni, spaghetti, mixed vegetables, mushrooms and one more can of beef broth. Simmer until pasta is cooked. More liquid can be added for desired consistency; this also works great with goose and chicken broth. Serve with soup crackers, garlic bread or bread sticks.

Edwin R. Motis
Tonopah, Nevada

GOLDEN GOURMET FOWL

4 servings of grouse, duck, pheasant, dove, chicken, quail, or venison, elk, antelope, caribou or bear
1 cup flour
1 tsp. black pepper
1 tsp. salt
2 T. paprika
½ cup margarine or butter
1 can cream of chicken soup
1 can cream of celery soup
1 can cream of mushroom soup
1 cup water

Mix flour, pepper, salt and paprika in a bowl. Coat meat in flour mixture and brown with butter or margarine in skillet over medium heat 7-10 minutes. Combine soups and water and pour into choice of cooking pan. Add browned meat and bake at 250° for 3-4 hours. Check at 1 hour intervals, adding water as necessary to maintain liquid. Serve over mixture of white and wild rice or top with dumplings. Serves 4.

Brian J. Mrnak
Park Rapids, Minnesota

WILD DUCK ROLLUPS

8 duck breast fillets
1 T. seasoned salt
1 box chicken flavor instant stuffing mix
8 strips bacon
8 toothpicks

Make stuffing as instructed on box. Pound duck breast flat, but not too thin. Sprinkle with seasoned salt. Place 1 tablespoon stuffing in the middle of each breast fillet. Roll up and wrap a slice of bacon around each one and secure with a toothpick. Place in baking dish with ¼ cup of water in the bottom, cover and bake at 325° for 1 hour.

Sue Miller
Saint Paul, Orego

Curtis Ericks

GOOSE JERKY

1	lb. goose breast, slived thin
2	heaping tsp. of Tender Quik
1	T. Worcestershire sauce
1	cup water
1½	T. liquid smoke

Mix ingredients listed above and place in ziploc bag. Soak for 1½ hours. Bake directly on your oven rack for 5 hours at 250°. Be sure to check often so it doesn't dry out too much.

Curtis Ericks
Rapid City, South Dakota

WILD GAME AND WILD RICE CASSEROLE

- 1   wild goose breast
- 2   chopped onions
- 1/4   lb. butter or margarine
- 1/2   cup white rice
- 1/2   cup wild rice
- 2   cups chopped celery
- 1   can mushrooms
- 2   cans cream of mushroom soup
- 1   can water

Soak wild goose breast in salt water overnight. Cut goose breast into bite-size pieces and brown in butter with onions. Mix remaining ingredients in oven proof dish and add meat. Cover and bake at 325° for 1½-2 hours. Leave uncovered last 15-20 minutes to brown. Chicken, turkey, beef, or pork may also be used. Serve with salad and garlic bread. Serves 6-9.

Robert W. King
Elyria, OH

SLOW COOKER DUCK

This is more a way to cook duck rather than an exact recipe. The beauty is that you can vary the ingredients according to your own tastes, or depending on what you have on hand.

2 small or 1 large puddle duck (teal, woodie, mallard, etc.)
1 medium apple, quartered
1 bay leaf
1 small onion, quartered
1½ cups medium dry wine
1 generous dash poultry seasoning
1 pinch each savory, thyme and rosemary
   other spices and seasonings to your taste
½ stick margarine
4 T. orange marmalade
2 T. currant or elderberry jelly

Wash and clean fowl and place in slow cooker. Add next 7 ingredients, apple through seasonings. Cook on low heat until meat is done and has loosened from the bone. Remove from heat and let cool. Remove the meat from the bone and cut into pieces no larger than one inch. Combine margarine, marmalade, and jelly in a frying pan; add meat and cook until meat is thoroughly heated and coated with the jelly mixture, stirring occasionally. Serves 2-3.

Bruce K. Flewelling
Rochester, Vermont

DEEP FRIED GOOSE FINGERS

1-3   lb. snow goose or other goose breast meat
3   cups flour
2   T. salt
2   T. pepper
2   T. garlic powder
2   T. basil
3   eggs, beaten
     oil for frying

Cut the meat into ½ inch strips. Combine all dry ingredients in a 1-gal. plastic bag. Dip the meat strips in egg, then place a few at a time in the bag and shake well. Place the strips in a deep fryer with enough oil to cover the meat. Cooking time is approximately 5-7 minutes. at 350°.

Charles Richards
Los Lunas, New Mexico

GRILLED GOOSE STEAK

3-5   lb. snow goose or other goose breast meat
2   T. or 2 cubes beef bouillon
1   tsp. salt
1   tsp. pepper
1   tsp. liquid hickory smoke
½   quart water, or enough to cover the meat
⅓   cup olive oil

Butterfly breast halves to make one steak each. Marinate steaks in bouillon, liquid smoke and water for 4-6 hours. or overnight. Remove steaks from the marinade and cover with olive oil. Add salt and pepper and grill for 10 minutes. per side or until done.

Serve with baked potatoes, salad or corn on the cob.

Charles Richards
Los Lunas, New Mexico

WATERFOWL WITHOUT ROASTING

4-6   ducks, goose, pheasant, quail, dove, woodcock
      or snipe
3   bags large egg noodles
4   26 oz. cans cream of mushroom soup
2   cups milk
      salt and pepper to taste

In a large pot, boil waterfowl until it's tender and falls from the bone. Remove waterfowl from broth and strain broth to remove impurities such as bone fragments and shot pellets. Return broth to pot and add sufficient amount of water to cook the noodles per directions on the bag. While the noodles are cooking, cut up the duck into bite-size pieces. Drain the noodles and add the cut-up duck and soup straight from the can. Stir in the milk, salt and pepper to taste. Simmer 20-30 minute, stirring frequently so the noodles don't scorch. Serve over mashed potatoes or alone. Serves a very hungry family of 6.

Brian Myers
Wheatfield, Indiana

BUCK'S SMOKED DUCKS

1   large duck per person   liquid smoke
    salt   brown sugar
    pepper   smoked sausage
    onion, quartered   bacon
    celery

Wash dressed ducks inside and out. Dry the ducks. Season with salt and pepper inside and out. Place a quarter of an onion, a 3 inch cut of celery and a 3-4 inch piece of smoked sausage in each duck cavity. Wrap 1-2 slices of slab bacon around each duck and secure with tooth picks.

Place ducks on foil; pour on liquid smoke and cover with brown sugar. Seal foil and bake at 325° for 2½-3 hours. Open foil and brown for the last 15 minutes Remaining liquid can be cooked down to make a gravy and served over rice.

Dave Buckley
Shreveport, Louisiana

BAKED DUCK AND VEGETABLES

2   whole ducks (8 to 10 doves may be substituted)
1   T. granulated garlic
2   T. Worcestershire sauce
2   T. soy sauce
1   T. parsley flakes
    pepper to taste
4   strips of bacon
2   onions, sliced
2   carrots, peeled and sliced
2   ribs celery, chopped
1   cup fresh mushrooms, sliced
1   bell pepper, cut into strips
    potatoes
    paprika, to taste
    salt, to taste

Cut slits in duck breasts and place breasts in pan. Sprinkle with garlic,
Worcestershire sauce, soy sauce, parsley and pepper. Place strips of
bacon across ducks. Put onion, then other vegetables on top of ducks.
Sprinkle with salt and paprika. Cover and cook at 250° for 4 hours. or
at 300° for 3 hours. Other vegetables may be added if desired. Serves 4.

Kenneth Pyka
Pattison, Texas

WILD GOOSE STROGANOFF

1	large onion
1	large green pepper
1	can mushrooms (pieces and stems)
5-6	cups goose, cooked ad cut up
2	cans cream of chicken soup
2	cans water
2	T. chicken granules or base
16	oz. tub sour cream; less if you do not like a sour cream taste

Sauté onion, green pepper and mushrooms until soft. Add remaining ingredients. If too thick, add water for a creamy stew look. If too watery, add a little corn starch to some water as a thickening. Serve over cooked noodles or rice. I like to make my goose the day before in the oven on a low heat, 300°, till it's tender. Stuff the goose with cut-up apples and onions. It takes the wild taste out of it. I never bake a goose on a rack because it gets too dry; always put it in a roaster with water and onion so it steams.

Harley D. Swanson
Underwood, North Dakota

GANDER NUTS AND GRAVY

1 goose, skinned and ground
1 large egg
  salt and pepper to taste
1 cup cooked rice
1 can cream of celery soup, cream of chicken,
  or both
1 cup chicken bouillon
  flour and water to thicken

Mix ground goose, egg, salt, pepper and rice into small meatballs. Brown in skillet and line in bottom of roaster pan. Mix cream soup and bouillon and thicken with flour to make gravy. Completely cover meatballs with gravy and bake in covered roaster at 325° for 1 hour. Best served over rice or egg noodles.

Mike Livingstone
Cheyenne, Wyoming

MIKE'S FAMOUS GOOSE AND GRAVY

1 skinned goose
1 cup mushrooms, sliced
2 cups celery, chopped
  salt and pepper to taste
1 can cream of mushroom soup, cream of celery,
  or both
  water
  flour to thicken gravy

Salt and pepper goose. Add 1 inch of water to bottom of Dutch oven and bake, covered, at 275° for 2 hours. Remove bird and cool. Shred goose from bones. Add mushrooms, celery and cream soup to drippings and thicken to gravy with flour. Add shredded goose to gravy and bake 1 hour or until tender. Excellent dished over egg noodles, rice or biscuits.

Mike Livingstone
Cheyenne, Wyoming

BETTER TASTING GOOSE AND WATERFOWL

A trick to better tasting goose and water fowl is to soak the birds in a salt brine solution for 1-2 days in the 'fridge. Change water frequently and soak till most or all of the blood is removed. I guarantee, it'll taste a lot more like goose or duck and a lot less like liver.

Mike Livingstone
Cheyenne, Wyoming

GRAPED GOOSE

1	goose
1	cup grape jelly
3-4	slices bacon
1	cup water
¼	tsp. salt
¼	tsp. fresh cracked pepper
2	T. cornstarch

Fill cavity of goose with bacon; salt and pepper goose. Put in slow cooker and add water. Melt jelly and pour over entire goose. Cover and cook for 8-10 hours. on low temperature. Remove goose from slow cooker and thicken liquid with corn starch either on top of stove or in slow cooker. Pour gravy over sliced goose.

Janet S. Oursler
Jessup, Maryland

TEAL STUFFED WITH RED CABBAGE

10	teal, cleaned (cordova teal are very small)
1	medium head red cabbage
1	lb. bacon
1	small onion, coarsely chopped
2	cloves garlic
1/4	cup red wine vinegar
1/4	cup brown sugar
2	cups dry red wine
1	tsp. cracked black pepper
1/2	tsp. celery seed
1	tsp. caraway seed (optional)

Save 10 slices bacon to wrap the teal; dice the rest and fry until half done. Add the onion and garlic and cook just until fragrant. Add the cabbage, vinegar, sugar, wine and seasonings and stir to mix.

Turn the heat to low, cover, and braise 45 minutes. Remove the cover and cook on high, stirring constantly, until most of liquid has evaporated.

Cool. (This step can be made up to two days ahead. Keep refrigerated.) Stuff the teal with the cabbage and place remaining cabbage in a shallow casserole, just big enough to hold the teal in one layer. Wrap each bird in bacon and place atop the cabbage.

Bake at 400° for about 25 minutes, until bacon and teal are dark brown and crispy. These can also be wrapped in foil and thrown into the fire, with the remaining cabbage heated in a saucepan. We eat these with our hands, sucking out the stuffing and letting the juices run down our chins. I once saw a 90-year-old woman at an outdoor cookout with one in each hand and a look of pure rapture! Serves 4-6.

Andi Flanagan
Kodiak, Alaska

BROWN'S DUCK STEW

2-3 lbs. duck breast
2 T. vegetable oil
½ cup flour
1 can cream of mushroom soup
1 packet beef stew seasoning
2 cups water
5-7 potatoes
4-6 carrots
½ cup onions, chopped

Clean duck breasts and cut in cubes in a large skillet. Heat vegetable oil. Coat the duck breasts in flour and brown them. In a slow cooker, add mushroom soup, seasoning packet, cut up vegetables, and browned duck breasts. Cook on low for 10-12 hours and enjoy.

Mark and Anne Brown
Taylor, Michigan

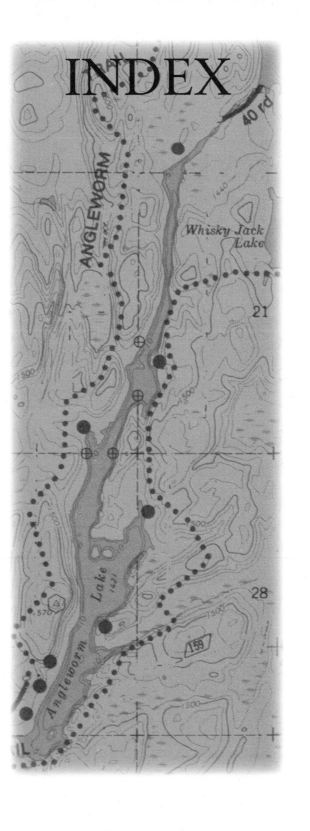

INDEX

H

I

J

K

L

S

W